OVERCOMING
ADDICTION

Register This New Book

Benefits of Registering*

- ✓ FREE accidental **loss replacement**
- ✓ FREE **audiobook** – *Pilgrim's Progress,* audiobook edition
- ✓ FREE information about new titles and other **freebies**

www.anekopress.com/new-book-registration

*See our website for requirements and limitations.

OVERCOMING
ADDICTION

A Biblical Path Towards Freedom

ELIZABETH SHARTLE

We love hearing from our readers. Please contact us
at www.anekopress.com/questions-comments with
any questions, comments, or suggestions.

Overcoming Addiction – Elizabeth Shartle
Copyright © 2018
First edition published 2018

Scripture quotations are from the ESV® Bible (The Holy Bible, English
Standard Version®), copyright © 2001 by Crossway, a publishing ministry
of Good News Publishers. Used by permission. All rights reserved.

Cover Design: Natalia Hawthorne, BookCoverLabs.com
Cover Photography: Aleksey Stemmer/Shutterstock
eBook Icon: Icons Vector/Shutterstock
Editors: Bronwen Jorel and Sheila Wilkinson

Printed in the United States of America
Aneko Press – *Our Readers Matter*™
www.anekopress.com
Aneko Press, Life Sentence Publishing, and our logos are trademarks of
Life Sentence Publishing, Inc.
203 E. Birch Street
P.O. Box 652
Abbotsford, WI 54405

SELF-HELP / Substance Abuse & Addictions / General
Paperback ISBN: 978-1-62245-517-1
eBook ISBN: 978-1-62245-518-8
10 9 8 7 6 5 4 3 2 1
Available where books are sold

Contents

Who Am I and Why Should You Listen to Me?

M y name is Elizabeth Shartle, and I'm a licensed clinical counselor. (I'm also an attorney, but that's not relevant here.) I've been a counselor for almost a decade, and much of this time has been spent working with adults with addictions and chemical dependency, usually co-occurring with other mental health disorders.

I firmly believe that, as they say, no one cares how much you know until they know how much you care, so I pray your reading further will assure you that I do care very much and that most of what I write is coming from a "been there, done that" point of view. I'm not just some fancy professional who's read about the problems that people have but never experienced any real difficulties herself. I've struggled with alcohol, cigarettes, over-eating, and other unwise choices. On the upside, I've been blessed to see alcoholic family members come into a saving faith and be granted the strength to set aside alcohol in favor of the joy of living according to God's plan. And on the downside, I've been pained to see bitter, angry family members reject God's plan and continue to use drugs, alcohol, food, sex, gambling, and more to escape the hurt we all experience in some way. So you can see why counseling would interest me.

I earned my counseling degree through Liberty University's distance learning program. At the time I registered, I figured they wouldn't want me as a student if they knew I was a cigarette-smoking, temper-challenged, single mom with a shaky faith. Little did I know! Enrolling in that counseling program was the first step towards immeasurably increasing my faith.

Initially, I thought I would counsel teenagers, since my own experience of being a teenager had been pretty rough. The Lord, however, had other plans. He led me to work in an outpatient treatment center for older adults with addiction problems. I loved the work, the clients, the sheer joy of seeing that ray of hope turn into action when a client came to understand and believe that it's never too late. Yet as my faith grew, it became more and more frustrating not to be able to say to them, "You don't just need faith in a so-called higher power. You need Jesus. He's the only one who can truly help you. Before it's too late, you need to come to a saving faith in Jesus Christ."

This desire to share my faith continued to grow, and then the opiate epidemic slammed into Ohio like a gale force wind. That's when I felt led to go to law school – with a focus on health law. And in my final year there, the Lord asked me to think about what it would have been like if I'd been able to show my counseling clients how the Bible and secular research on recovery fit together seamlessly. As a counselor, I'd spent years facilitating an intensive outpatient treatment group (IOP), a program designed to help someone who's early in recovery learn skills for living life without addiction. I'd seen for myself just how closely those skills match what Scripture tells us about how to live life and treat one another. What you're reading now is what you might call an IOP handbook thoroughly backed up by the

Word of God, our Creator. This is what I would have loved to have shared back then and this is what I offer to you now.

I believe God allowed me to work first with older adults, so that I could see clearly how an entire life can come close to being wasted in pain and suffering and addiction. Addiction can lead to divorce, broken families, failed health, joblessness, homelessness, and death.

It doesn't have to though. Addiction can be overcome. My life hasn't been a shining example of good Christian living, but my Lord Jesus Christ has given me – as he gives to all who confess him as Savior – gifts to use to build up the church, which is the body of Christ. (These gifts are as described in more detail in 1 Corinthians 12:8-10; Ephesians 4:7-13, and Romans 12:3-8.) The Lord promises that all things will work together for good for those who love God and who are called according to his purpose (Romans 8:28). This means the mess of my past and the past of others I've known becomes a message of grace and mercy that I can share with you; likewise, the mess of your own past can be redeemed, and you can use it to help others in turn.

> **Addiction can be overcome.**

The Lord is allowing me to draw upon my education, my personal experience, my professional experience, and most importantly, my understanding of Scripture to write to you. With his blessing, I pray these words will ring true, touch your heart, and stir your soul to faith and freedom in overcoming addiction.

Chapter 1

The Beginning

This book is meant to be read like a letter. You'll notice, for instance, that I casually switch from talking about "you" to "we" or sometimes "I." That's just my way of showing that we're all in this together. I don't pretend to have all the answers; I just write in faith, trusting our Lord will guide my words and use them for your benefit and his glory.

The tone is meant to convey the kind of interest a good letter conveys. "Hey, heard you were having a rough time and just wanted to let you know I was thinking of you. I'd like to share some things that I've learned. Things that have helped me out over the years. Mostly, I want you to know I believe you can get through this."

Addiction isn't the easiest subject to discuss, but here in these pages – in today's language – it is what it is. If we can talk about it for what it is, then it may seem more possible to do something about it.

Not that everyone necessarily finds talking easy. Take my mother, for example. She never finished high school, so I'm not sure she knew quite what to make of it when, in elementary school, I was enrolled in a class for gifted kids. But when I realized my vocabulary exceeded hers, I began to put my thoughts into plainer words, because I never wanted my mom to feel dumb when she talked to me. If you use big words that make people feel dumb, they tend to not listen to what you have to say. I wanted my mom to want to talk to me, so I did everything I could to make that happen.

Using plain words instead of elaborate ones means that to some people – in fact, to quite a few people – I come across as simple, and they feel that way about the things I'm led to share too. But that's okay. I'm in good company, because the apostle Paul talks about this in 1 Corinthians 2. He says he didn't come proclaiming the gospel with what he called *lofty speech* because then it would seem like man's wisdom instead of what it really was – the wisdom of the Holy Spirit. Much of what I say will seem very simple. It will also seem counter to the wisdom of this age. Paul speaks of that, too, in the same chapter of 1 Corinthians. The wisdom of God was imparted long before we were born and has nothing to do with what year this is. God's wisdom is timeless. *There is nothing new under the sun* is as true now as it was then (Ecclesiastes 1:9). There have been people with addictions for almost as long as there have been people at all.

God's wisdom is timeless.

You can research any concept I discuss and study it in all its complex detail if you wish, and you'll find the depth of knowledge you seek. Please be careful though. The wisdom of men is foolishness to God, and Scripture is filled with paradox (1 Corinthians 3:19). Things seem upside down at first glance, or concepts seem opposite but are linked together. Let me give you some examples. Jesus says the least shall be greatest and the last shall be first (Luke 9:48; Matthew 20:16). He also says whoever finds his life will lose it, and whoever loses his life for

Jesus's sake will find it (Matthew 10:39). The saved in Christ are both saints and sinners (Ephesians 2:19; Romans 3:23). The power of God is perfected in weakness (2 Corinthians 12:9). All those statements seem pretty contradictory, don't they? So if the words I write go against what "everybody says" about addiction and mental health and you wonder about this, then talk to someone whose faith is biblically based and strong. Someone who knows their Bible, loves the Lord, and loves you too. Don't just rely on human wisdom, because the ways that seem right to man lead to death (Proverbs 16:25).

For now, I'm going to start with a personal story, and if you can relate, then I hope you'll trust me enough to read all the way through. (If you're frowning and muttering, "I don't care about *your* life, I care about *my* life. Just tell me about over-coming my addiction," you can go straight to chapter 2. But I hope you won't, for the reasons I give in the next paragraph.) I figure that if I share a little about my experience, it may seem safer to keep reading. It will be, as much as a book written by a stranger can be, as if we're in this conversation together, by choice. It's important that it feels like that because we'll get to some parts that are painful to consider, but vital to recovery.

It's also important to read all the way through because I write the way I talk. I might be in the middle of explaining a concept and then switch to a by-the-way comment, but you'll find that I pick up where I left off. If you jump around and skip pages when you read this, you'll miss a lot of stuff that I believe the Holy Spirit has led me to share with you. I could organize this better, but then it wouldn't feel like a conversation or even a letter. It would read a lot more like a textbook, which I tried to write at first. It was boring.

So. Here's my story. Maybe you'll see yourself reflected in some parts of it.

I grew up in the church, and I had some experiences with

people who didn't meet my young ideas of what a Christian ought to be. First, like I said, I was in a "gifted" class at school. That tends to set you apart. I was also chubby, and I dressed funny. Many of my nicer outfits came from my Aunt Betty's closet. She was eighty years old. A lot of popular kids went to my church, but I wasn't one of them. I was the chubby, weird kid who didn't say much except to answer questions I knew the answer to. So, as far as I could see, none of that brotherly love Christians were supposed to feel for each other was coming in my direction.

One thing that did come in my direction was a hymnal. With a hard cover. I was ten years old, alone in the Sunday school classroom, playing the piano while waiting for the teacher or other kids to come in. Some boy I didn't know came into the room behind my back and slammed a hymnal into the back of my head so hard that I pitched forward and saw stars for a moment.

Another thing that came in my direction in Sunday school was the pain inflicted by a different boy – someone I actually knew from school. This time I was reading a book while waiting for the others to arrive. A group of kids came in, and this one boy came up behind me, grabbed a fistful of my hair, and yanked it. Hard. Then he scratched two lines into the back of my neck with his dirty fingernails – lines so deep they bled. Then he sat down with his friends, laughing. All of them laughing. I was eleven.

I didn't tell anyone. My dad had already lectured me that taking a book to Sunday school was rude and would make others think that I was unfriendly and unwilling to talk. I don't think it ever occurred to him that book or no book, the other kids didn't talk to me. I figured if I said anything about being attacked, it would be twisted into being something I deserved or brought on myself. I don't recall ever telling my parents about something bad happening that wasn't turned into somehow being my fault.

It took a couple of decades for me to understand we blame victims as a way of not having to deal with the idea that things don't always make sense. We blame victims because we don't like to think we, too, are vulnerable to being harmed at random. We blame victims to keep alive the illusion of order. And sometimes we blame victims because otherwise we'd have to face the guilt of knowing we failed to protect them. My parents apparently worked on the theory that people act sensibly, which meant that if I'd suffered, I must have done something to bring the suffering upon myself. There was no allowance for the possibility that sometimes, for reasons beyond our comprehension, sad and even hurtful things happen to people who've done nothing to cause or deserve them. If you identify with that, try reading the book of Job. You'll find comfort there. Job's friends thought pretty much the way my parents did, and they didn't hesitate to tell him so.

> We blame victims because we don't like to think that we, too, are vulnerable to being harmed at random.

Around the time that I was dealing with being attacked in church, my father became increasingly ill. For months I thought he had tuberculosis, because that was the only thing I'd heard anyone discuss. Finally, a family member told me he had cancer. Their tone suggested I ought to have known, but how could I? For one thing, I was still a child, and for another, we didn't discuss unpleasant things in my family, or at least not beyond basic facts.

For instance, although I knew that my father had been married before, we never talked about those marriages or the mothers of his children (my half-siblings, but much older than me and my two sisters). In the same way, when my half-brother and his wife were getting a divorce, my mother said, "Do you know what divorce is?" I said yes. She said, "Well, that's what's going on with your brother and his wife, now." I said okay. And that's the last time we talked about it.

Or take what happened when my unmarried sister got pregnant. She was ten years older than I was, had moved out two years earlier at age seventeen, and lived a few cities away. I never even knew she was pregnant. I'm not sure how much time passed after she gave birth before I was told I had a nephew, but even after I knew of his existence, he was another subject we never discussed until (surprise!) he came to live with us for a while. I was so jealous of the attention he got, and I felt almost abandoned in comparison. I felt guilty for being glad when he was gone and when he came back years later, I felt guilty all over again for resenting his return. I've read before that sibling rivalry is what happens when kids feel they must compete for too little amounts of love and affection. I believe that.

Anyway, when my father began to lose the battle against lung cancer, I didn't see any point in trying to discuss it with anyone in the family. Instead, I approached the youth director at church. I asked him if he knew my father was dying. He said yes. I said I'd like to talk to someone about it. He said I should talk to his wife. She was an elegant, polished woman who'd never shown me much warmth. Their son was one of the most popular boys in school. How could she possibly understand? How could I find the words to explain to her what it felt like to be unattractive, unpopular, and unwanted? The idea of sharing anything with her was just – no. I didn't trust her with my heart or my feelings or my secrets. I mentally added the youth director to my list of people in the church I couldn't trust.

What my youth director didn't know was that it wasn't just that my dad was dying. I threw that out as an opener. It seemed a serious enough topic that the likelihood of not being offered some help would be slim. Misjudged that one. But the real problem was that I was feeling selfish and sin-sick. When my dad was in the hospital and my mom stayed over, I stayed with my half-brother or my half-sister. Staying with my half-sister meant riding the bus. Riding the bus meant getting picked on for being the chubby, weird girl and trying to find a kindly face that would allow me to sit next to them – all the general horrors of riding a bus when you're not liked. But being concerned with this when my father was dying made me feel like a horribly small, petty person.

So I spent the summer wandering around town and avoiding my bed-ridden father who lay dying in the back bedroom. I had no way to judge whether avoiding him made me the worst, most selfish, most awful person in the world or whether it was okay because it often seemed he and my mom – in fact, my whole family – didn't want me around anyway.

My dad was sixty when I was born. He retired at sixty-five while my mom continued to work. (He was quite a bit older than she was.) For the next few years, she'd get off work at four o'clock, we'd have dinner at four-thirty or five, and shortly afterwards my mom would go to her bedroom to lie down, usually with a cool washcloth over her eyes and forehead. I'd get a few minutes to talk to her washcloth-covered face before she'd tell me to go. At that point, I could go out to the living room and watch television with my father so long as I didn't try to talk to him and interrupt his shows. If I didn't want to watch TV, I could sit in my bedroom and read. I know that at the age of nine, I was still being told to go to bed at eight o'clock. There were many nights when I wasn't tired, but I had to pretend to be asleep when my parents went to bed, or I'd be in trouble for being awake.

Was this every single night? No. There were Sunday night Disney movies that I got to watch on the TV in the back bedroom, sometimes even with a snack. There were times when my mom would come out of her bedroom and play a board game with me. Or sometimes she'd head out to the kitchen and call me to share a bowl of ice cream or a bagel with her. These were seriously treasured moments.

Looking back through adult eyes, I can see that my mother was in an appallingly difficult situation, as she tried to juggle the demands of her job, her terminally ill husband, her household chores, her young daughter, and her relationship with the older children. I think, though, there were many nights when I justifiably felt unwanted after being told to either go away or be quiet.

When I realized just how sick my dad was, I tried to make a deal with God. You see, I knew I ought to get baptized. I was attending a Baptist church after all, and getting baptized is what you do when you claim to believe Jesus is Lord and Savior. You believe that, and you get baptized. Simple. The idea of being full-immersion baptized was uncomfortable though. Me by myself in front of the church, in water, trusting the pastor not to drop me during the dunking part, getting dunked, having water splashed on my face. It all sounded very unpleasant, so I'd postponed it.

But now I thought perhaps if I got baptized, God would let my dad live a little longer. I knew by this point that he was going to die. I just thought maybe I could have a little more time. So I signed up to get baptized during an evening service.

Well, the day didn't go exactly as planned. First off, while I was wandering around the neighborhood as usual, avoiding the father that I didn't want to die, I encountered a flasher. Running home in fear, I felt God was showing he was angry with me on a day I'd thought he might be pleased with me. Failed again.

The baptism was even worse. When I got to church, the woman helping in the changing room told me to hang my clothes on the hook and put the white robe on. When the ceremony was over, I climbed the stairs out of the baptism pool feeling pretty good. I'd gone through with it; the pastor hadn't dropped me; the words he'd spoken had been very moving. Then I got back into the changing room, and the helper stared for a moment. "You didn't wear a bra?!!!" Whatever good feeling I had evaporated. She was disgusted. Appalled. I was ashamed. I was twelve. I didn't know.

I continued going to church on Sundays though. At that age, I didn't really have a choice. On Wednesday nights, I went to youth Bible studies at a different church.

One evening, the Wednesday night group leader announced that those who completed a certain number of lessons could go on a trip to Buena Vista. It sounded exciting – ninety minutes away but a whole other world of sights and attractions. As the time grew closer though, I think I got sick. Anyway, there was some reason I didn't complete the last lesson, so I had no expectation of going on the trip. I didn't complain or say anything to the youth leader; I just didn't get the permission slip signed.

The night before the planned trip, the youth leader called my mom and got verbal permission for me to go on the trip. When my mom told me, I was surprised. I told her I didn't think I was allowed to go. We figured the youth leader must have changed her mind because I was so close to achieving the goal, and it hadn't been for lack of trying that I didn't complete the last lesson.

It was a great trip. I felt included – an incredibly rare feeling for me. There were four of us girls plus the youth leader. We walked all over and saw the sights, and on the way home we all sang songs together. I was really grateful to have gone.

The next Wednesday when I got to group, the leader said, "Elizabeth, I need to speak with you." I got that hollow-stomach, I'm-in-trouble fear. We stepped outside. She said, "I can't believe you let me take you to Buena Vista. You didn't complete all the lessons."

Bewildered, I said, "I know. When you called my mom, I thought you'd changed your mind."

"Do you know what a lie of omission is?" she snapped. She told me she was ashamed of how I let her grant me a reward I didn't earn. She said I'd cheapened the reward for everyone who did earn it.

At that point, I was done with the church and everyone in it. I had not one shred of respect for anyone in authority there. I felt ashamed and humiliated and angry. I still didn't know if I had somehow brought these things on myself, but I wasn't about to try to discuss it with anyone. If I couldn't trust the people who are supposed to love Jesus and love each other, then who could I trust?

I never went back to the Wednesday night meetings, and my mom never said anything about it. Like I said, we didn't discuss much in our family.

Then, shortly after I turned sixteen, in eleventh grade, I had a crisis of faith that drove me to seek some kind of answer. The guy I had dated in tenth grade (yes, I was finally socially acceptable enough to get asked out – well, by one person, anyway) had graduated and joined the army. I felt abandoned. He had only signed up for two years, but that was an eternity. I had no long-term perspective. He was the first person that had ever seemed to like me for me. He seemed to want to know my thoughts, my interests, my plans. He was the first person who listened without getting squirmy and looking like he'd like to get away, but then he left me anyway.

I cut class that day and went into the high school auditorium to play the piano. A boy came in. No, this one didn't cause me physical pain. But when I awkwardly tried to leave, he grabbed my hair with one hand, held my face, and plastered a choking, disgusting wet kiss on my mouth. I left school and drove downtown, where there was an Episcopal church, a gorgeous building. I just wanted to go inside and pray and ask God, "Why?" But it was locked.

The parsonage was next door. The minister's wife found me in uncontrollable tears and invited me into her kitchen to talk.

I'm sure it would've been helpful if I could've said something like, "The church has let me down. It's a place where I've been randomly attacked, I've been shunned, I've been shamed, I've been humiliated, and I don't understand why. I don't know how to make it stop because I'm almost always alone; no one ever wants to spend time with me; the only person who did has gone away. Soon I'll go home to my mother who's told me she thinks I'm odd and my nephew who now occupies all of her attention – attention that I got for such a very short time. I'm sixteen years old, and I'm tired of living life, feeling unwanted and unloved and too weird for people to deal with."

> "I've been shunned, I've been shamed, I've been humiliated, and I don't understand why."

But I was an inarticulate, sobbing teenager. I'm not sure what I said, but she responded by telling me God loved me.

Oh. Okay. Yeah. But that's just words.

She was a nice woman, but I don't remember anything else she said.

Fast forward four years. I wasn't in college, but I was living in a college town. I drank almost every night and had no idea that most people don't black out when they drink. I honestly thought blacking out was normal and just went along with drinking. Mind you, I wasn't twenty-one. All my drinking was under-aged and illegal. I smoked cigarettes, a pack a day, and occasionally marijuana. I was in a live-in relationship with a controlling, abusive guy. After a few months, he decided we should separate and reconsider our relationship. Before he left, he raped me. He ripped my clothing to shreds, smashed my possessions, and left me with a burst ear drum and bruises all over my body. But at least he finally left.

A couple of nights later, I met a group on campus hosting a Christian rock music event. There was still enough southern Baptist in my soul to be disturbed by the idea of Christian rock, but the people were very nice. They invited me to church, offered to give me a ride, and even presented me with a Bible. One woman in particular was so kind and wanted so much to reach me. At some point in our conversation, while I was in a flood of tears just as I'd been with the minister's wife, she said, "Jesus loves you."

Ri-i-i-i-ight. The guy who just beat me up and raped me used to say he loved me too. Just words. Pretty much the same words the minister's wife had used, and I had no idea what either of these women really meant. I'd already spent considerable time thinking about how no one could possibly love me because no one actually knew the real me, and I didn't trust anyone enough to let them know the real me.

The concept of love was baffling. God loves me. Jesus loves me. Oh really? Why would they do that? I got the impression that both the pastor's wife and the college campus woman thought I couldn't believe I was loved by the Lord because I felt I wasn't worthy of being loved. I was pretty sure they were on the wrong track, because it seemed to me that it was more a case of being unwanted than being unworthy. But looking back, I realize I was so out of touch with my emotions back then that I can't say for sure whether I felt worthy or unworthy of love.

What I did know was that God was supposed to love everyone. I'd gone to church all my young life, so worthy or not, I knew God was supposed to love all people more or less the same. I also knew people who had done worse things than I had. I knew people who were violent, people who were drug dealers and thieves. I thought, logically, if God loves everyone, then God ought to love me too, because I wasn't as bad as those people were.

But all this knowing didn't touch my heart. I didn't *feel* loved. This love that God was supposed to have for me might have saved me from going to hell, but it didn't save me from myself. It didn't keep me from the pain of hurting myself or being hurt by others. I wasn't even sure what being loved would feel like.

I know now, as an adult, what really says *love* to me is when you pay enough attention to what's going on in my life to be willing and able to do something you know will make my life easier. I realized this when reading Gary Chapman's *Five Love Languages*.[1] If you're willing to do acts of service for my benefit, that says love to me. If you know I don't have time to get groceries and you volunteer to stop at the store for me – wow! You do love me! But that's me. Others feel loved when you spend time with them doing something they enjoy or when you express appreciation or affection or come bearing gifts. I also feel loved when plans are made and kept. When a friend shows up happy to see me, it feels like love.

Because I'd never had a consistent relationship like that in my life, because I didn't read the Bible, because I didn't pray, and because I'd stopped going to church, there was no way for me to understand what it was supposed to mean when I was told that God loved me or Jesus loved me or they both did or do or whatever.

I certainly didn't think there was anything very appealing about me, even where God was concerned. Like I said earlier, by the time I enrolled in Liberty University's counseling program, I wasn't sure they'd even want me as a student if they knew

---

1   Gary D. Chapman, "Love Language #4, Acts of Service," *The Five Love Languages: The Secret to Love That Lasts* (Chicago: Northfield Publishing, 1992), 91-104.

me. I didn't enroll because I wanted a degree from a Christian university; I enrolled because it was the only distance-learning program I found that promised licensure. It was the only way I could work full-time, pursue my degree part-time, and still survive as a single mother. The classes I took required me to read my Bible of course. But they also required me to consider my faith and how my worldview impacted me as a person as well as how it would impact me as a counselor.

I'd always hesitated to read the Bible all the way through because I figured it would just spell out all my flaws and make me feel even worse about myself. Also, I knew people who I assumed read the Bible, and it didn't seem to do much for them, so why should I expect it to do anything for me? What I never imagined was that reading my Bible would ignite my love for and my unending gratitude to God the Father, Son, and Holy Spirit. I never imagined it would change my bitterness towards others into greater compassion for them and greater understanding of how flawed all of us are. But somehow, miraculously, that's what happened.

I'm not saying it happened in a blinding flash, but day by day, reading my Bible and praying, I learned to take God at his word. If you knew a guy you could really trust and he said, "I've found a great deal on a car," you'd be excited if you were shopping for a car. Right? Well, I came to realize I could take God at his word and understood that no matter how many times people let me down, I could still rely on him. I became excited about the future, as I'd never been before. I saw that I could leave behind my addiction to cigarettes and booze and look forward to what God had in store for me. Yes, people fail. All the time. But God never fails us. He says, "Trust me," "Don't be anxious," "Love one another," and "I give you my peace." He's always in control, even when he allows us to do foolish and hurtful things.

Trusting him, I learned to pray when I was anxious. I learned to shift my thoughts into words like "God's got this. I don't need to worry." I learned to pray for wisdom as to what I should do. I learned the freedom of forgiveness. When something bad happened, I could ask the Lord to search my heart and tell me if I'd somehow contributed to the situation, so I could ask forgiveness. I prayed to handle changes with grace and dignity. I became a better friend, mother, and sister because I could be a better person for the Lord than I could be for anyone else. I learned that having peace is being able to accept whatever is happening – almost immediately – and then praying about it rather than wasting time and energy on *if only* and empty wishes.

> "God's got this."

When I started to read my Bible regularly, I still held a lot of bitterness inside, more than I'd ever realized. One of the last classes I took at Liberty included an exercise that involved writing a story of our own. A group of us was sitting around a large conference table, writing our stories as instructed. Tears began to fall – not just my tears, but tears from others in the group also. I looked up and caught the eye of the woman across from me who was, I think, in her late fifties. She said, "This stuff never goes away, does it?" The stuff she was referring to is the stuff of pain and regret and loss and shame and loneliness. Classic themes that are often woven into our life stories. In theory, we were a group of well-educated, insightful people ready to go out and help everybody else solve all their problems – as though we had none.

That's just it though. We've all got problems. Lord knows. And it doesn't always take a lot to bring them to the surface.

And what does all this have to do with addiction? Or you?

Well, there's some stuff everybody knows, whether they're well educated or not. Right? Stuff like you shouldn't drink to excess or smoke or do hard drugs or gamble or fritter away your time with internet porn or pursue illicit sex or shop on credit or eat fried food.

I'm not convinced everybody knows why not. I think often the underlying idea is that you shouldn't do these things because the Bible says not to. The Bible says it's a sin, end of story. If, like me, you've struggled to understand what it even means that God loves you, then the fact that the Bible says "Don't do this" doesn't touch your heart. It may be that you've tried to be good only out of fear of going to hell if you aren't. Like me, you may not realize God's love can save you even from yourself.

I'm not convinced everybody knows how to make good choices and what true spiritual and physical health even feels like. Don't get me wrong; physical health is great. But this isn't a flesh-and-blood kind of fight; it's a spiritual battle. *For we do not wrestle against flesh and blood, but against the rulers, against the authorities, against the cosmic powers over this present darkness, against the spiritual forces of evil in the heavenly places* (Ephesians 6:12). And in the midst of this spiritual battle, addiction whispers, "It's not worth it. It's not worth the effort of trying to stop. No one cares. Nobody loves you."

If I'm not sure I want to spend another day on this planet, then why would I choose a nice healthy salad for lunch over the wings and mozzarella sticks? The fried food is going to clog my arteries and possibly cause a heart attack. Woohoo! Bring me a second plate. Cigarettes burning my throat and lungs? Sure. Why not? Statistically speaking, girls without fathers tend to seek the love of a flesh and blood man in grossly unhealthy ways, and I was pretty much the poster child for that particular statistic.

But it doesn't have to be that way. I know how much God loves me, how much Jesus loves me, for *God shows his love for us in that while we were still sinners, Christ died for us* (Romans 5:8). Jesus says if we don't love him then we can't even love God;

whoever hates me hates my Father also (John 15:23). If I know the rules in my Bible were breathed out by my almighty Creator – that changes everything. Since he created me, he knows what will bring me love, joy, peace, patience, and more (Galatians 5:22-23). The rules aren't meant to spoil all our fun. They're set down for his glory, for our good, and always, always to bring us and others closer to him. God's Word is deep and multi-layered and complex, but the message is simple. God's love can save us even from ourselves. God's love isn't just about how we spend eternity; it's about how we can live joyfully today. And we can trust him. Always.

Maybe if we can talk about how God made us in his image, what that means, and how it plays out in our everyday lives, we can better come to terms with what damage addiction has done and how we can undo it.

With love, maybe we can talk about something that's painful and difficult. We can agree on a plan that makes sense for lessening our pain, leaving our addiction behind, and living as God designed us to live. When you understand more of how and why you were made, how the rules are designed for your benefit and God's glory instead of being invented to limit your joy in life, then it becomes easier to leave addiction behind.

Chapter 2

Our Search for Pleasure

The apostle Paul wrote to the church in Philippi:

Finally, brothers, whatever is true, whatever is honorable, whatever is just, whatever is pure, whatever is lovely, whatever is commendable, if there is any excellence, if there is anything worthy of praise, think about these things. (Philippians 4:8)

The key to freedom from addiction is to think about things that are lovely.

That's it.

That's it?

You mean just focus on the rainbows and not the rain? When life hands you lemons, make lemonade? Turn that frown upside down?

You can't be serious.

Sayings like this used to get on my last nerve. I was so often angry and bitter. Life was one frustration after another, and the idea that you could just snap your fingers and just like that see the best in every situation was nuts. No way would this solve my problems.

The truth is that it may not often be easy to think about things that are lovely, but beauty and pleasure are critical to our existence.

How do I know that? Because our heavenly Father made us in his image, and he appreciates beauty and pleasure. He created them after all. And if our Creator appreciates beauty and pleasure, that means we are created to appreciate beauty and pleasure.

Truly.

Our heavenly Father obviously designed us to appreciate the beauty of the world he made. He designed us to appreciate a cool breeze after a soft rain. He made the mountains, oceans, stars, and flowers. He designed sex for committed marriages. He made snow and lightning bugs and green grass.

He made food! Genesis 2:9 tells us, *And out of the ground the LORD God made to spring up every tree that is pleasant to the sight and good for food.* God first made food grow on trees that were pleasing to the sight. In other words, food came from beauty. The fuel that human bodies needed was based in a thing of beauty to be food for our soul as well.

The food part best helps illustrate this point about our basic desire for pleasure.

Think about hunger. When you're hungry, I bet your main desire is not a fruit-flavored, soy-protein, diet bar. But what if that was nutritionally complete? What if you knew for a fact it would fill you up and satisfy your hunger? Would it be your first choice? Second? Would it be what you ate only if there was nothing better to eat?

If you would only eat it when you had nothing better to eat, what then constitutes *better*? Something that tastes good? Aha!

That you would want to eat something that tastes good suggests you would prefer your food to be pleasurable.

Now – what's your favorite meal? Maybe it's a half-pound cheeseburger with loaded fries. Maybe you're a bit more refined and would prefer eggplant parmesan with a side of steamed asparagus. Baby asparagus even.

Let's say it's a steak. (My apologies to vegetarians. Please try to envision a Portobello mushroom, steakish meal.)

So steak, baked potato, and super fresh, crisp salad.

Where do you want to eat? On a patio? You grilled the steak yourself so you know it's perfect. The day is beautiful and sunny, 78 degrees, just turning dusk. Mosquitos are divinely absent on this gorgeous evening. Or maybe you're at your favorite steak house. There's a candle burning on the table and . . .

Who's with you? Someone you love? Someone you're excited about being with and want to impress? Someone you want to thank or celebrate with?

> Our heavenly Father obviously designed us to appreciate the beauty of the world he made.

Someone whose company you enjoy, at any rate. A person who also enjoys a great steak dinner, certainly. Not someone who whines and complains about everything and sends the steak back twice. No, not that person. Someone pleasant and positive who will appreciate dinner. That's who you want to eat with.

From fruit-flavored, soy-protein, diet bar to steak dinner with someone who's a joy to be around.

Eating is not purely about the body's desire for food. Eating is also about pleasure. When your stomach growls and your brain sends out the "I'm hungry" message, it's a reminder that your body would like some food, preferably some enjoyable food. A whole enjoyable food-consuming experience, in fact.

Now imagine you don't get the enjoyable company. Okay, you can still enjoy a good meal by yourself. You'd probably rather enjoy it on your own at home than on your own in a restaurant though. A lot of people dislike eating alone and would especially prefer not to eat alone in public.

What if you had to eat your steak with plastic utensils? Oh. That's not a pleasant thought. Hmmmmm – how sharp is the plastic knife? Maybe you'll go for it if the plastic knife is at least useful enough to kind of saw through the steak. Yeah, that wouldn't be too bad if the steak's tender.

What if you had to eat your dinner with plastic utensils on a Styrofoam plate balanced on your knees? What if you had to eat your dinner with plastic utensils on a Styrofoam plate balanced on your knees in the middle of a busy bus terminal with everyone brushing past you? What if you're trying to eat your steak on a Styrofoam plate balanced on your knees in the middle of a busy bus terminal, and a stranger moves in close and stares at you while you eat? Okay. All righty then. We've left the realm of enjoyable meal – yes?

It's frustrating to know what would be enjoyable, to have something that could almost be enjoyable, and yet to be unable to enjoy it.

The addicted brain knows this, too. That's why it will urge you into greater and greater depths of depravity to get the same high you once got from just a little bit of nothing. The addicted brain wants the pleasure it once had – and more. That's why overeating becomes an addiction as well. The pleasurable taste and texture of good food leads to a desire to consume, a desire to feel satisfied that isn't quenched in the way God designed. The addicted brain wants to maximize pleasure and minimize pain, and it has become set in the ways that seem to lead to this goal.

This is why your only hope of a sober life has to involve intentional, God-given, and God-honoring sources of pleasure. The addicted brain has to be retrained to function in the way our Lord designed.

Addiction has perverted the God-given desire for pleasure in this life and turned it into a clanging, unceasing frustration with life itself, because the pursuit of pleasure outside of God's design will never fully satisfy.

Recovery – living a life without addiction – means accepting the God-given and God-honoring sources of pleasure as sufficient. It means learning to live according to God's design even though that will never make sense to the unsaved world. It means training your brain to reject the lie that you need more and more and accept the truth that you can live in joyful contentment with less and less.

Am I saying that everyone needs to live as poor as a church mouse? Fortunately, no. All I'm saying is that a limited income doesn't have to mean that you only have a limited amount of happiness in your life, any more than having an unlimited amount of money guarantees you unlimited happiness. To a large extent, it depends on what you do with what you have. *As for the rich in this present age, charge them not to be haughty, nor to set their hopes on the uncertainty of riches, but on God, who richly provides us with everything to enjoy. They are to do good, to be rich in good works, to be generous and ready to share, thus storing up treasure for themselves as a good foundation for the future, so that they may take hold of that which is truly life* (1 Timothy 6:17-19).

> God himself is where we find our hope and joy and treasure.

What is *that which is truly life*? It's placing our hope in God who provides everything for our enjoyment. It's being rich in good works and being generous. Obviously, God knows about our search for pleasure, and He's created the path for us to reach our goal. *God himself* is where we find our hope and joy and treasure. Pursuing God is nothing the world suggests we ought to do, but it's truly living life.

So how does this work? How do you go from the darkness and despair of addiction into the bright light of God's love and his design for living?

Chapter 3

Mind Control

I think many of us believe we our thoughts are our own. Not true.

So whose thoughts are they if not ours?

Aliens! Aliens put those thoughts in our head!

No. Put down the tinfoil hat.

Our thoughts are influenced by a variety of factors. The healthy brain can take in a lot of information, sift through it, separate the wheat from the chaff (that is, what's good from what's useless) and learn and grow.

In addiction, though, this doesn't happen so much. Addiction results in all-consuming thoughts of whatever we're addicted to. There's not a lot of learning and growing taking place.

For example, a shopping addiction can lead to hiding new purchases from loved ones, putting credit card statements out of sight, and scheming about how to get enough cash together to pay the bills. There's a preoccupation with new versus old or with the last piece of a set or maybe a limited-edition item. There might be guilt when there's no money to put in the church offering plate. There might be rationalization: "The church doesn't need my money." There will definitely be a pervasive desire to shop. And shopping online is double the gratification. You don't have the downside of wearing yourself out walking the stores; instead, you have two upsides. There's a perceived reward in the pointing and clicking, and then there's a second reward when the item arrives. All that anticipation is very difficult to stop thinking about and looking forward to, if you're fighting the battle on your own.

A shopping addiction isn't all that different from a drinking addiction, although many people would like to think it is. The person with a drinking problem thinks about drinking. They want to drink, and they'll get very, very unhappy if something interferes with the time they've set aside for drinking. It doesn't matter whether this time is the four hours between work and bedtime five days a week or the twenty-four out of forty-eight hours on the weekend; the time for drinking must not be disturbed. If the time for drinking *is* disturbed, it's usually because there's some darn family event going on where it would be inappropriate to show up drunk. The alcoholic then has to decide whether to hold off on drinking, show up anyway, or pass on the invitation. As the drinking addiction progresses, passing on the invitation happens more and more often.

What happens next reinforces the addiction, whether it's an addiction to shopping, drinking, using drugs, or some other behavior. If you turn down family events in order to pursue your addiction, pretty soon your brain has accepted as fact that family members greatly interfere with the pleasure of using alcohol or other drugs or otherwise indulging in addictive behaviors.

Family members become kind of annoying. They get in the way of pursuing your addiction. That's especially true if they're bold enough to say something about your habits. Friends who speak up about missing you or say you haven't seemed like yourself lately are the next casualties of your addiction. The pleasure of indulging is too precious to the addicted brain to be ruined by a kill-joy who doesn't understand.

The thing is, the brain is so cunning. Whatever you've been telling yourself to justify the addictive behaviors will get more and more believable. You will create (if you aren't already creating) the situations your addicted brain uses to justify continuing with the addiction.

A shopping addiction isn't all that different from a drinking addiction.

Do you *need* a drink because you've had a stressful day? Chances are you'll continue to have more and more stressful days, and you won't even notice that the bar for what is stressful has become lower and lower.

Do you need a hit because it's humid and your bad knee is acting up? Pretty soon that doggone knee will act up on clear, sunny days with zero humidity.

Do you need to get to the bingo hall, casino, heroin dealer, mall, race track, bar, liquor store, out-of-the-way motel, crack house, or pornography site?

Are you telling yourself you deserve this treat? reward? break from stress? way to blow off steam? release from physical pain? temporary relief from emotional pain?

What is your brain telling your mind in order to justify continued use and behavior?

Because whatever it is, it will narrow your thoughts and behavior and focus; if you manage to keep a job, your life will consist of nothing more than you and your job and your addiction.

Our brains require balanced chemistry in order to feel a variety of emotions and learn new things. Addictions, on the other hand, throw our brains so far out of balance that learning and loving don't take place. It doesn't matter whether the addiction is to a substance, a process, a drug, or a behavior.

The brain chemistry is wrecked when we indulge in pleasures beyond those God designed for us to enjoy.

Addiction changes the brain, and as the brain changes, the addiction itself and all its associated behaviors are reinforced.[2] When addiction begins to take over, it doesn't leave much room for anything new. All the thoughts and behaviors become very set, very rigid, very ingrained. The way the brain works allows an addiction to be reinforced.[3]

How exactly does this happen?

Let's consider some examples.

On a good day, when I'm feeling warm and happy and blessed to be alive, if someone cuts me off in traffic, I can say, "Oh! My word! Heavenly Father, I hope that person doesn't cause an accident and hurt anyone."

But on a bad day, when I'm tired and running late and dreading my appointment (which is probably why I'm late) and someone cuts me off in traffic, I'm not about to say a prayer for them. Most likely, I'm saying, "That ignorant so-and-so deserves to get in an accident," followed almost immediately by, "Oh, heavenly Father, please forgive me for that rude and angry thought."

When I'm in the grocery store and feeling blessed to have money for food, and I hear a toddler whining, I think, "Oh, poor baby sounds tired."

But when I'm feeling impatient waiting in the express line with one item while everyone else is using all the do-it-yourself scanners for entire carts full of groceries, and then a toddler starts whining – well, let's just say my response isn't likely to be "Oh, poor baby."

---

2   D. Belin et al., "Addiction: failure of control over maladaptive incentive habits," *Current Opinion in Neurobiology* 23, no. 4 (2013): 564-572, OhioLINK Electronic Journal Center, doi:10.1016/J.CONB.2013.01.025.

3   S. H. Ahmed, M. Graupner, and B. Gutkin, "Computational Approaches to the Neurobiology of Drug Addiction," *Pharmacopsychiatry* 42 (2009): S144-S152, OhioLINK Electronic Journal Center, doi:10.1055/S-0029-1216345.

So our thoughts are influenced by present circumstances, and if our present circumstances are good, that makes it much easier for us to have pleasant thoughts. When things are going well, it's not hard at all to follow the apostle Paul when he said, *whatever is true, whatever is honorable, whatever is just, whatever is pure, whatever is lovely, whatever is commendable, if there is any excellence, if there is anything worthy of praise, think about these things* (Philippians 4:8). God wants us to think about what's true and lovely.

However, if our present circumstances are full of stress and fear and anxiety and irritability (especially when life interferes with addiction), it becomes difficult to think about anything pleasant. In fact, one of the hallmarks of addiction is looking forward to using or indulging in your drug or activity of choice. If that's what you most look forward to in life, then everything else becomes a kind of annoying distraction that you just have to get through until you can get to what you enjoy most. Your thoughts will reflect your annoyance with life in general and all the things that are interfering with your addiction in particular.

I refer to a drug or activity of choice because most people have an addictive drug or behavior they prefer to all others, and sometimes two or more are combined. People can also switch addictions – from cigarettes to chewing tobacco, from alcohol to Ativan, from crack cocaine to crystal meth. You get the picture.

What's more, if you feel a sense of loss in giving up your addiction, it's often hard to see the rest of life as making up for this loss, even if you gave up your addiction because it was killing you. People in pain tend to focus on their pain, and the pain of losing your preferred form of escape will make you very irritable. The everyday annoyances of life will feel huge.

Yet we are told to rejoice. *This is the day that the LORD has made; let us rejoice and be glad in it* (Psalm 118:24).

In the grip of active addiction, that's a tough thing to do.

What else is going on?

Bodily processes influence our thoughts.

When my stomach growls and the thought "Oh! I'm hungry" comes into my mind, that's not a controlled thought. I didn't decide at that moment to think about hunger. (Most people don't *decide* to think, "I'm hungry," unless they have an eating disorder.) When a bodily process is the source of the thought, the thought comes to the brain unbidden, uncontrolled, and unasked for – especially if you're in a situation where, for example, there's not going to be any food for a while. Certainly, that would be a time when you don't *choose* to think, "I'm hungry," because it's decidedly inconvenient to be thinking about food when there's none coming.

Another example. If I go to take something out of the oven, using a thin potholder, and I forgot to clear the top of the oven earlier, so that I could set the dish down, and now the pan is burning through the potholder – ow! I didn't *choose* to think, "Oh, that hurts!" The fact that I'm being burned causes my brain to send a signal that comes out in words like *Ooh, ow,* or *ouch!*

Our thoughts are influenced by bodily processes, and this absolutely includes the bodily processes that accompany addiction. Alcohol and opiates are obvious sources for physical addiction as well as for psychological addiction. As brain science continues to develop, we see less and less distinction between *substances*, such as alcohol and opiates, and *processes*, such as gambling and shopping, as far as the addictive potential and brain chemicals are concerned.

While it's true that alcohol and opiate withdrawal can cause death if not properly managed, it's not true that there's nothing physical associated with other drugs or activities. Gamblers crave the adrenaline rush.[4] Frequent use of marijuana is associated

---

4   Michael Dieter Egerer, "And that is where the fun ends – General practitioners'

with altered brain waves and thyroid function issues.[5] Crack addicts can experience stomach cramps and bloating; they may pass gas in anticipation of getting high. Smoking crack also may have life-threatening effects on the digestive system.[6] Sex-related addictions and eating disorders have a physical basis.

These physical processes accompany addiction and influence your thoughts. As with hunger, the bodily processes alone are capable of generating certain thoughts.

The thought "I'd really like to get high" may come into your mind two days after you swore up and down you were done. The bodily processes themselves, separate from your own will or desire or determination, will create thoughts of how desirable indulgence would be.

Truth doesn't flow from the desires of my flesh.

This is the main reason that it's important to understand we don't choose our thoughts unless we choose, to the extent possible, to choose them. It's very important to understand this. Our brains are wholly capable of generating thoughts from a variety of influences and sources, and it takes diligent practice to immediately recognize and set aside the thoughts that keep us locked in addiction.

Your body will influence your brain to throw out the thought that drinking, drugging, or surfing the net is a good idea. If you believe this automatically generated thought and act on it, you reinforce the addiction. My body and mind will work together to tell me that half a chocolate cake is a good thing to

conceptualization of the line between recreational and problem gambling," *Nordic Studies on Alcohol and Drugs* 32, no. 1 (2013): 31-47, ISSN: 1458-6126.

5   R. I. Herning, W. Better, J. L. Cadet, "EEG of chronic marijuana users during abstinence: Relationship to years of marijuana use, cerebral blood flow and thyroid function," *Clinical Neurophysiology* 119, no. 2 (2008): 321-331.

6   Alok Tiwari, Mohammed Moghal, and Luke Meleagros, "Life Threatening Abdominal Complications Following Cocaine Abuse," *Journal of the Royal Society of Medicine* 99.2 (2006): 51-52.

have for dinner. I know this isn't true. Truth doesn't flow from the desires of my flesh.

What else influences our thoughts? Expectations.

Most people who are addicted will constantly expect the worst. Depending on the addiction, it might always feel as though you're waiting for the other shoe to drop. Disaster lurks around every corner. Any day now you're going to be found out, and when that happens – boom! The hammer comes down.

And this thought process doesn't let up in other situations. It's not like you're skulking around at night, thinking about how close you are to ruin, then waking up all bright and cheerful in the morning. You're not hiding *just* your addiction while you're ready to be an open book to your loved ones; you're also hiding the thoughts and expectations that relate to your addiction.

Your expectations reflect your frequent thoughts about the probability of being found out, or losing a loved one, or finally running out of money, or whatever the ultimate consequence of your addiction may be. Your thoughts will be poised to expect the worst. That's not just because of addiction. Our default setting as humans is to be negative and critical. Expecting the worst is an extension of our normal state, and addiction merely exaggerates it. Logically, you can't sneak and hide without thinking about and mentally preparing for being caught.

When you always expect the worst, you can't trust, and you can't *be* trusting. Expecting the worst prevents you from being vulnerable with others, because allowing yourself to be vulnerable requires you to trust the other person. When you can't risk making yourself vulnerable, you can't fully enjoy loving relationships. If someone finds out what you've been up to, they're going to be – angry? hurt? sad? furious? vengeful? all of that and more? So you keep your heart in check to prepare for the worst while trying to act as though everything is fine.

What an exhausting show to put on! How much energy is left in your heart and mind for caring deeply about your loved ones?

Our thoughts are also influenced by planning and fantasizing.

All of us can intentionally turn our thoughts to certain subjects or scenes, reminisce about past times, or mentally relish hopeful details of a time yet to come, but the addicted brain in particular likes to hang out here. Problem is, it doesn't settle for plans and fantasies about loving relationships. When not using, the addicted brain likes to fantasize and plan for when the use or activity can begin again. This is very common and even necessary to continue the addiction when it involves more planning than a run to the corner store.

The addicted brain absolutely knows that planning for indulgence is necessary. I've known people who could plan a drug purchase for vacation two months in advance and yet forget to reserve the hotel room. This isn't a coincidence or an accident. It's the result of the narrow, powerful focus of the addicted brain.

The addicted brain likes fantasy and planning, particularly planning how to obtain more of the desired substance. Or planning the next shopping spree or gambling weekend or adulterous encounter. The addicted brain rolls around in this fantasy and planning to a great extent. These thoughts can be both chosen thoughts and unwanted thoughts that rise up on their own.

It's very important to realize the addicted brain acts under the influence of the addiction. Thoughts are not chosen unless we choose to choose them. Even then, we'll only be marginally successful without committed practice.

Exercising mind control, controlling our own brains, takes serious effort.

When you stop thinking that your thoughts are *you* in some set way and start to realize they're a function of your brain and bodily processes, you'll realize why the apostle Paul said, in Romans chapter 7, that he could tell bodily pleasures aren't controlled by his reason. He knew sin had such a hold on him that he couldn't just will himself to do right, for he said, *I know that nothing good dwells in me, that is, in my flesh. For I have the desire to do what is right, but not the ability to carry it out* (Romans 7:18). When we understand this, it's easier to understand why Scripture says there's no one who is righteous; no one at all (Romans 3:10).

We're incapable of willing ourselves to do only what God says is right. Why? Because we're inherently sinful – not just those of us who are addicted but all of us, every last one. We're creatures of the night who will pursue endless pleasure if given half a chance. Ideally, we'd like to pursue endless pleasure in such a way that no one gets hurt, and we still have great relationships, but if someone does get hurt, we can find the most remarkable ways to justify it. We're slaves to this sinful nature of ours, and it propels us in ways we never expected.

Maybe you're uncomfortable with the concept of sin. Maybe you think you've met good people. People who aren't as bad as you are. As I am. People who don't seem very sinful. You've met upstanding citizens who work hard and take care of their families. They give to the poor and go to church and mow their lawn regularly. Yes, there are lots of fine people like this in the world, but they're still human, which means they're still sinners. God sees their hearts, and *the heart is deceitful above all things, and desperately sick* (Jeremiah 17:9). Outward appearances do not a good person make.

If you can come to terms with the idea of being sinful, then you can be a lot more grateful for Jesus. If you can accept the idea that your body and brain will move towards sin no matter how much you try to reason, will, or talk yourself out of it, then you can begin to come to terms with the depth and extent of your need for Jesus.

Trying to control the thinking of the addicted brain is like continually trying to straighten the steering wheel when you've got a bad tire with low air and have needed an alignment for months. The wrestling is constant. There doesn't come a point where you "win" and are able to drive straight without effort. The same with trying to control the thoughts in an addicted brain. It's a never-ending struggle.

Again, the apostle Paul knew this. He said we *take every thought captive to obey Christ* (2 Corinthians 10:5). To take a thought captive means to understand that our thoughts are going to stray and lead us into enemy territory if we don't capture them.

> When you seek the Lord, you seek to be known and loved by your heavenly Father who created you.

This is why we're told to think about the things that are pure and lovely and praiseworthy. If you manage to stop thinking about your addiction, then you've got to have good thoughts to replace the negative ones, so there's no room for them to come back into your brain.

It is very important not to dwell on thoughts of using and fantasies of indulging in your addiction. Because of the way our brains are created, it's important for us to say, *"Your face, LORD, do I seek"* (Psalm 27:8). Thoughts of using are thoughts of seeking instant gratification, thoughts of changing the way you feel – this instant. When you seek the Lord, you seek to be known and loved by your heavenly Father who created you. Understand that thoughts of using do *not* arise from wonderful, unique you; they're the thoughts of the flesh, which has been broken by sin. Instead of allowing those thoughts opportunity, you can seek the Lord, who promises healing, cleansing, steadfast love, and mercy (Proverbs 4:22; Titus 3:5; Nehemiah 9:31). *The Lord is good to those who wait for him, to the soul who seeks him* (Lamentations 3:25).

It takes daily, even hourly, practice to wrestle your thoughts away from fulfilling your desires. Effective mind control shifts your thoughts to seeking the Lord instead, but it's not easy, especially at first.

So how do you go about seeking Him?

Chapter 4

Knowing that God is Good

Once you were not a people, but now you are God's people; once you had not received mercy, but now you have received mercy. (1 Peter 2:10)

What does it mean to be God's people?

Well, if you were talking about a group of people that you were willing to claim and you called them my *peeps* or my *crew* or my *homies* or some such phrase, what would it mean?

People who are God's people know that God's got their back. With him being our heavenly Father, Jesus Christ being the author and perfecter of our faith, and the Holy Spirit being our guide, we're good to go. God's on our side. And *if God is for us, who can be against us?* (Romans 8:31).

Suppose you're a person in the grip of addiction, and you tried to quit, but it didn't go well.

Scary.

Really scary.

You said you're done, that's it, no more, never again – and it didn't work. You said you're absolutely cutting back, only certain times, certain situations, very, very limited – and it didn't turn out that way. You couldn't control it.

You didn't like having to come to terms with not being in control. No one does. A person doesn't have to have an addiction to dislike not being in control.

Out of control. A drug, habit, or a behavior is propelling you in unwanted ways.

What do you do about it? Well, instead of saying, "Wow, I've got myself into a situation here that I can't control," you say, "I had a good tip – that horse should have won!" You say, "I know if I get drug tested, I'll lose my job, but this job sucks anyway." You say, "I just had to have those two-hundred-dollar shoes."

Deep down, you know none of this is true, but the reality is – if you're in a situation you can't control, and you can't stop, and especially if you've hidden it – you'd rather claim to have made poor decisions than throw yourself on anyone's mercy and say, simply and sincerely, "Please help me. I can't help myself."

If you've gone through substance abuse treatment before and it didn't stick, then it's even worse. You took the plunge, swallowed your pride, threw yourself on the mercy of the court or the community treatment agency or your loved ones and then started using again. You lost control. Now it seems there's no hope. You tried. It didn't work.

Try again. Please try again. You were created with a purpose. You were created to find fulfillment in a personal relationship with Jesus Christ, our Savior, and to experience something far greater than bottomless pain. You were created to experience fathomless heights of joy – yes, joy! – in service to our Lord. You weren't created to trudge through sobriety any more than you were created to sneak and slither in addiction.

Chances are that there are people who love you much, much more than you know. Maybe they don't show it in ways you need, but that can change. Maybe you feel completely alone, and it seems like no one loves you. Maybe your belief in God is faint. God is like your father on a bad day, but fortunately up in the sky and too far away to harm you. Is that how you see him? That's not the Christian God. If you think it is, please read the Bible. It's God's love letter to us. Read how he wants the best for us. Read how he wants to bless us. He wants you back. He wants you as you are right now, in this very moment. Read and pray that our heavenly Father will show you this and make it clear to you.

This is part of what it means to seek the Lord. It's so much easier to seek God if you believe that he's good. God's plans are always better than any plans we can make. God's will for our lives is always better than what we think will make us happy. God desires to bless us. God is good. God can be trusted.

God's plans are always better than any plans we can make.

Believing God is good and can be trusted is faith. Believing he showed his goodness and love for us by having his only begotten Son pay the price for our sin is faith. Reading the Bible because it's God's Word is an act of faith. Going to church because God's Word tells us not to neglect meeting together is an act of faith (Hebrews 10:25). When we do what God tells us to do through the Holy Spirit, we're stepping out in faith.

Know that God isn't an employer who hands out a paycheck (blessings) based on the number of hours we put in, though. Jesus talks about this in Matthew 20. He describes a situation where workers have agreed to work in the vineyard for a set wage. Later, more workers agree to work in the vineyard. Still later, even more agree to work. Obviously, the last ones worked for quite a short time while the first ones worked all day. Those who had worked all day thought they should be paid more. That's only fair. Right? But – *Am I not allowed to do what I choose with what belongs to me? Or do you begrudge my generosity?*

(Matthew 20:15). God gives to us generously, and he forgives us generously, regardless of how much or how long or how often we've sinned. If we compare our status to someone else's, we lose perspective. The comparison itself is wrong.

When we fail to see that the Lord is good, we forget the depth of the sin he's forgiven us. When we fail to see he's good, we think someone else got something they didn't deserve or we're being unfairly punished. In our bitterness and resentment, we become incapable of being happy for someone else, and we think God isn't good or just or fair. Too many of us have thought, "I've been good, so why did this happen to me?" or "I've been praying, why isn't this situation fixed?" or "Why did this good Christian get cancer?" and "Why is this young child so sick?" Why, why, why?

In Job 38:4, God challenges Job's attitude with the question, *Where were you when I laid the foundation of the earth?* After a long series of similar questions, God asks in Job 40:2, *Shall a faultfinder contend with the Almighty?* Faced with the knowledge of his own limitations, Job rightly responds, *I lay my hand on my mouth* (Job 40:4). In other words, the Good Lord is Lord of all. He says he is good and his love endures forever (Psalm 100:5). If we can't believe this, we have an idea of God that's based on something we made up in our own minds.

We have free will. So do others. By the grace of God and indwelling of the Holy Spirit, we can control our behavior, but we have no control over the behavior of others. We can control our actions, but we can never control the outcome. The entire world – not just some people, but the whole world – groans under the weight of sin that separates us from God (Romans 8:20-22). The weight of sin in the world shows up in death, disease, and disaster, and we know too well how sin shows up in our own lives.

Poor decisions are the consequence of being a slave to sin

and not seeking and trusting God. Have faith in Him. The Holy Spirit will lead you step by step to a life worth living, if only you'll allow him to. It won't be a life free of pain and sorrow, because the world is full of sinners who do hurtful things, and the world itself is broken by sin. But the Holy Spirit will lead you in a life that's joyful and fulfilling despite pain and sorrow. It may be difficult to imagine how this will work, but that's because God's ways aren't our ways. In the book of Isaiah, we read, *For my thoughts are not your thoughts, neither are your ways my ways, declares the LORD, For as the heavens are higher than the earth, so are my ways higher than your ways and my thoughts than your thoughts* (Isaiah 55:8-9).

If you want to be free of addiction, you've got to be honest and brave. You've got to be *willing* to be honest and brave. Honest and brave. *For God gave us a spirit not of fear but of power and love and self-control* (2 Timothy 1:7).

Being brave doesn't mean being fearless. It means taking action despite our fear.

Being honest doesn't mean telling everyone under the sun your personal business. What it does mean, though, is being honest with God and yourself. When we confess sin, we're not telling God anything he doesn't already know, but admitting our wrongdoings lets us move closer in our relationship with him.

Have you ever lied? Of course you have. Well then, you know the tension that exists when you know you're lying and you think the person you're lying to knows you're lying? When you lie, naturally it erodes the other person's trust in you, but when you think someone knows you're lying and they keep quiet, it erodes your trust in them to be truthful as well. Both of you are engaged in deception and game-playing, which is not the basis of a trusting relationship.

That's more or less how it works with God too. We're forgiven when we confess our sins and trust God to do what he told us in his Word that He would do – forgive us. *If we say we have no sin, we deceive ourselves, and the truth is not in us. If we confess our sins, he is faithful and just to forgive us our sins and to cleanse us from all unrighteousness. If we say we have not sinned, we make him a liar, and his word is not in us* (1 John 1:8-10).

By denying our sin, we fail to trust God to forgive us. This failure to trust leads us to believe God can't be trusted. What a terrible, vicious circle. The solution is to be brave enough to trust him – no matter what. We need to realize that if the Good Lord says he is, in fact, good, we have to trust him and take him at his word, because we can't ever see the whole picture of how our lives intersect with others, which means we have to rely on his perspective. Either we trust or we drive ourselves mad trying to control what was never within our ability to control in the first place.

> The solution is to be brave enough to trust the Lord – no matter what.

Jesus is the way, the truth, and the life. The truth will set you free, and God made us free to enjoy God-honoring sources of pleasure, because he's good and he loves us. If you can step out in faith, you can experience this for yourself. You will *taste and see that the Lord is good* (Psalm 34:8).

So, believing God is good, seeking him, and purposefully trying to keep good thoughts going are all things that we should be doing.

The world says, "How naïve. What utter nonsense. Foolishness! It's totally ridiculous! You must keep your guard up, keep your friends close but your enemies closer, and keep a sharp eye on everyone, because you can't trust anyone these days."

But if you're following God's design for living life, then the Holy Spirit, not the world, is guiding you. Our Lord has promised to give us all things that pertain to life and godliness, so we might be *partakers of the divine nature* (2 Peter 1:3-4). We don't become as God, but his Spirit gives us the knowledge we need for living. Reading the Bible and knowing its contents prepares us for living *that which is truly life*. We don't need to hang on to all the negative things from our past or insist on keeping a suspicious eye on others. Neither are we to be naive or intentionally ignorant. We are to rely on and trust God so we might have peace and noble thoughts.

How do you find things to think about that are pure and lovely and commendable when you're used to thoughts filled with doubt and distrust? And why bother? Because the God of our Salvation says to, and we have faith he knows what he's talking about because he made us. So, making a conscious choice to choose good thoughts and having faith that God is good, let's set out.

Chapter 5

Finding Beauty

Y ou need beauty in your life. We all do.

Beauty is essential. God made us in his image to appreciate beauty, music, food, companionship, and laughter. He tells us we know him by seeing and experiencing his creation. *For his invisible attributes, namely, his eternal power and divine nature, have been clearly perceived, ever since the creation of the world, in the things that have been made* (Romans 1:20).

So – what in your life is truly beautiful?

What do you take time to notice and appreciate?

What do you linger over? What moves you to tears?

Having or creating beauty in your life doesn't have to mean regular trips to art museums or opera performances. Beauty is in the eye of the beholder, but if you find beauty in an art museum or musical performance, you need to go. Why wait? Many communities have free concerts and free or low-cost days at the museum, so go ahead and soak yourself in beauty.

I grew up in south central Florida, and because I was never fond of the heat, I hated living there. Hated the roaches, the palmetto bugs, the "love-bug season," the mosquitoes, the fire ants, the sandspurs, and the chameleons. Ugh. Why, oh, why would anyone choose to live there?

Now, I realize there was a beautiful lake in our town within walking distance of where I lived. Palm trees against a starry sky have become synonymous with a coveted beach life. Now I'm older, I can admit the area was and is beautiful. In my younger years, full of bitterness and misery, I never appreciated it.

Finding beauty means literally taking the time to smell the roses. Do you have flowers in your yard? Is there a yard near you that has flowers? When it snows, do you see the light hit the snow like a thousand sparkling diamonds? Do you appreciate the ozone smell of a thunderstorm? Do you listen to music that stirs your soul? Do you sing? Never mind whether you sing well or not. The question is whether you find pleasure in singing, whether it satisfies something deep within. Do you draw or paint or have any creative outlet – even a coloring book and crayons? Even if you don't feel you're the creative type, do you live in a big city where there are street performers who can make you laugh or touch your heart?

Taking the time to find and appreciate beauty is the first, most basic step towards filling the hole that not using or indulging in your addiction will leave.

Taking the time to appreciate beauty will force you to slow down, breathe, listen, wait, and be still. It's the first step towards meditation, which has tremendous mental and physical benefits, but we're not there yet. Right now, we're just trying to figure out what you find beautiful that should give you a feeling of awe and wonder. It should make you feel a bit like a little kid.

Maybe you think your kids are beautiful. Maybe you think your spouse is beautiful. Or maybe you would if you said the words: My loved ones are beautiful – even if your loved ones are a dog or a cat. Beauty is everywhere. Or can be, if you know where and how to look.

If you're reading this like, "Okay, beauty. Check. Next!" Then slow down. You're missing the point. The point is beauty today, tomorrow, and always. Beauty to make you feel wonder again.

Beauty isn't optional or superfluous or an add-on. If it's raining and the sun is shining, you should be looking for a rainbow. Every time. If you're outside and the sun is setting, you should be looking for the sunset. If it's night, you should be looking for the moon and stars. If you're in a room full of people who are rubbing your nerves raw, you should look for a kindly face, a sign in the room that someone feels love. You should look for the beauty to focus on.

Do you sing? Never mind whether you sing well or not.

Beauty is to your soul what breath is to your body. It's essential.

I know there's a good chance you're reading this and thinking it's a bit light for the depth of your troubles. "Beauty, seriously?" Or perhaps you're a guy thinking everything I've named so far is so much romantic nonsense. That's okay. Maybe your idea of beauty is something more down to earth.

For instance, I have a friend whose idea of beauty is a well-crafted boat, yacht, or ship. He could watch them, look at pictures of them, be stirred to great depths of yearning by looking at boats all the livelong day.

Or take that time when I was walking around an art festival and happened upon a display of hand-crafted lamp shades so beautiful that they brought me to tears. Lamp shades! Who knew? Another time in my life, I was fortunate enough to visit the Philadelphia Museum of Art. The furniture took my breath away.

There are reasons why the idea of beauty seems too simple a way to begin filling the hole that addiction leaves behind. One big reason is that just as there's a huge diet industry because of the increasing rate of obesity, so there's a massive and expanding pharmaceutical industry developing around psychotropic drugs to counter addictions, obsessions, depression, and other such conditions.

In other words, if focusing on beauty were the first step towards eliminating an addiction, then you'd think these industries wouldn't be necessary and certainly wouldn't be growing at the rate they are. You'd think a lot more people would be talking about simple things to promote recovery – anything from visiting an art gallery to riding a powerful motorbike down a winding country road. Instead, we see ads for treatment centers in luxurious settings, not to mention commercials for new drugs with what seems like 250 side effects listed in the fine print or rattled off at high speed in the voice-over at the end of the ad.

In a way, it seems logical that there would be a great need for treatment centers and new drugs and the whole recovery industry, because people who are battling addiction can't very well do it on their own. But think about it, and pray about it, understanding this: *The fear of the LORD is the beginning of wisdom, and the knowledge of the Holy One is insight* (Proverbs 9:10). Do you think God would want you to have to go out and spend huge sums of money just to begin the process of dealing with addiction in your life? Considering the Lord created you in his image to appreciate beauty, do you think it's perfectly fine for you to ignore that aspect of the world he created for you to enjoy?

Logic isn't taught as it once was. When you read the Bible daily and begin to have a relationship with the living God through his living Word, you'll learn to reason things through. *For the word of God is living and active, sharper than any two-edged sword* (Hebrews 4:12). *Faith comes from hearing, and hearing through the word of Christ* (Romans 10:17). You'll learn to think, not in ways that make sense but in the way that makes the most sense. We ourselves are letters of the living God, and his Spirit is written on the tablet of our hearts (2 Corinthians 3:3). *Come now, let us reason together, says the LORD* (Isaiah 1:18). It's God's desire that we have wisdom, and while there's no doubt huge groups of people, businesses, and industries reject the Lord's wisdom, that's no reason for you to be the fool (read Proverbs) with *itching ears*, rejecting sound teaching (2 Timothy 4:3). God has made the wisdom of this world foolish (1 Corinthians 1:20).

The Lord says we're made in his image. He appreciates beauty and has incorporated beauty into this world and into our senses for a reason. There's no justification for ignoring this or assuming it's too simple to accomplish anything.

Many of the Bible verses about the beauty of the earth refer to God's glory and righteousness. For example:

The heavens declare the glory of God, and the sky above proclaims his handiwork. (Psalm 19:1)

He loves righteousness and justice; the earth is full of the steadfast love of the LORD. By the word of the LORD the heavens were made, and by the breath of his mouth all their host. (Psalm 33:5-6)

Out of Zion, the perfection of beauty, God shines forth. (Psalm 50:2)

He makes me lie down in green pastures. He leads me beside still waters. He restores my soul. He leads me in paths of righteousness for his name's sake. (Psalm 23:2-3)

For his invisible attributes, namely, his eternal power and divine nature, have been clearly perceived, ever since the creation of the world in the things that have been made. (Romans 1:20)

The concepts just naturally go together. Making it a point to incorporate beauty into your life is akin to adding God's own righteousness to your everyday existence. Prioritizing the beauty that God has set before us is prioritizing goodness, which is in opposition to the darkness and despair of addiction. Beauty and goodness go hand in hand.

WARNING! DANGER!

Because of who we are, because of our sinful nature, the experience of beauty can produce a powerful longing. It's important to realize this longing is for the fullness of life with God in eternity. True beauty will stir your soul, move you to tears, and give you the urge to create more beauty. You are, after all, made in the image of God, the ultimate Creator. It will make you want to possess beauty in your home, in your life, and in your everyday environment. You may feel this unquenched longing and call it sadness or despair.

You are, after all, made in the image of God, the ultimate Creator.

You must pray about this.

If beauty has been absent from your life for a long time, you may have no idea what I'm talking about. That's okay. Come back to this when you begin putting beauty in place and find your soul stirred with a bittersweet longing and restlessness that you have no place for. Then you know it's time to pray. Then you'll know what C. S. Lewis was talking about when he said, "It was valuable only as a pointer to something other and outer."[7] In *Surprised by Joy*, Lewis described this bittersweet feeling of longing and desire and concluded that it points us towards God, who is holy, and set apart. Beauty and joy should

---

7   C. S. Lewis, *Surprised by Joy: The Shape of My Early Life* (Harcourt, Brace, Jovanovich, 1956), 238.

be appreciated, said Lewis, in much the same way a signpost is appreciated when we're lost. Nowadays we might say we should appreciate joy and beauty the way we appreciate a functioning GPS – same idea. Beauty points us towards God.

Not only do beauty and God's goodness go hand in hand, but in seeking the beauty God has put around you, your brain shifts. Human nature is such that if unchecked, one of the first things we're going to seek is the desires of the flesh. The desire may be for food, sex, power, a reduction in our pain, the euphoria of being high, or a quick and easy escape from stress; we're always, always seeking something. We need to make sure, though, that what we're seeking is worth finding. Seeking to find and appreciate what's beautiful in your life shifts the addicted brain from self-seeking to outward-seeking. Beauty points us towards God.

One final note here on beauty. It's my personal belief, based not just on my own experience but on my observation of other people's lives, that making it a point to notice beauty, have and behold beauty, and appreciate beauty when it's around you has a more immediate effect than making a gratitude list or a list things to be thankful for.

Why?

Because we're sinful, fickle creatures. The person in ill health wishes to be in good health. The person in good health is thankful for the good health but wishes for more money. The person in good health and financial comfort wishes for more obedient children or a more loving spouse or more respect in the workplace. The person who has good health, a great family, and a job that confers respect and status will find themselves wishing for fewer everyday inconveniences. Whatever it is we have, we ought to be content; yet always, we wish for more. A gratitude list may be easy to create, but it rapidly becomes outdated.

The apostle Paul said, *I have learned in whatever situation I am to be content* (Philippians 4:11). He was writing from prison, yet he speaks of having learned how to be content regardless of his surroundings. It's a process. Therefore, I believe recognizing and seeking opportunities to appreciate beauty is a more immediately effective tool for lessening the pain of turning away from addiction. Beauty is recognized by all ages and provides God-honoring instant gratification. It will also give you much to be grateful for as you seek the Lord in his creation.

Chapter 6

A Good Meal

When you take the time to prepare a good meal, you send the message to yourself that your self is worthy of a good meal. You may have heard our bodies are a temple (1 Corinthians 6:19). To put this into practice, to treat your body as the place where the Holy Spirit dwells, means not only to give up the bad but also to bring in and celebrate the good as designed by God. You give thanks to your heavenly Father for providing the food in prayer, but you also give thanks by taking the time to enjoy it. Good food is always a gift to be enjoyed and appreciated.

Even if you're getting your food from church pantries and food banks, you can take time with meal preparation. If you work two jobs and don't have the time, you can ask those who live with you to join you in taking more care with meals. If you live alone, you can sit down while you eat; if you're in a shelter, group home, or residential facility, you can at least give thanks for the food.

Try to curb the tendency to criticize and find fault. Making the best of any situation is a skill, and a very desirable one.

Constantly criticizing is a sin, and being critical does nothing good for your state of mind. It is a common aspect of human nature, maybe even our default position, to be discontent and find fault. But it's important to resist this. Find something positive to say at every meal.

In the book of Numbers, Scripture tells us of twelve Israelites who were sent to scope out the land of milk and honey. Ten returned with a negative report that set the rest of the Israelites to grumbling. Those ten died, and because of their bitter complaints and disrespect for God, most of the rest were sentenced to wander the desert for forty years (Numbers 14:36-38). Grumbling has consequences. Perhaps not death and homelessness, but a loss of enjoyment in life itself is unavoidable.

We cause our own unhappiness and discontent with petty criticism.

If you're fighting addiction, part of your weaponry must include a renewed capacity for joy. You undermine your own joy by dwelling on what is lacking instead of appreciating what's present.

We cause our own unhappiness and discontent with petty criticism. Not long ago, I read about an exercise that suggested putting a rubber band on your wrist and snapping it whenever you realize, or someone points out, that you're being critical. A substitute plan was to put the rubber band on one wrist and try to make it through a day without having to switch it to the other wrist. In other words, no switching would be necessary if there were no words of complaint or criticism that day. I have to admit I haven't tried this trick. I don't think of myself as being particularly critical, but this exercise might show me something different. Maybe it's time for me to be brave and find out!

Beauty is essential. Food is essential. To the extent possible, combine the two. Set the table, use napkins, don't watch television while eating. Enjoy the meal. Enjoy the company you have for the meal. If you don't have human company, find something beautiful to put on the table while you eat, or play some beautiful music in the background. Resolve to make each meal as pleasant as possible and to enjoy it as much as you are able. Every meal. Every day.

In my early twenties, I had a fake rose in a bud vase on my kitchen table. I'd pour some apple juice into a fancy glass I got at a thrift store, and most often, I'd be eating my frozen dinner alone; but I took the time to make it nice – because I could. Because, although I didn't realize then how important beauty is, I wanted to enjoy my meal as much as possible. Going through the preparations and sending the message to myself that I was worthy of a good meal took away some of the loneliness of eating alone.

Now, before I go any further, I want to address a stumbling block I've had and have known others to have. I grew up with a reverse prejudice against anything too fancy, too hoity-toity, or too rich.

I'm addressing this now in case you may have a similar resistance to being anything but "plain and simple" or "the real deal" or "down to earth" or any other phrase that suggests you're not the kind of person to gild the lily or sugarcoat the truth or do anything besides being who you are – kind of, except for the addiction part.

God made us to appreciate beauty and food and music and companionship. If there's any part of you resisting what I've outlined, then I hope you'll take the time to figure out why the idea of beauty doesn't sit comfortably in your mind.

Often, people who don't want to "put on airs" feel their poverty like a toothache.

I was in Girl Scouts for a couple of years, and I sold Girl Scout cookies door to door. I remember my mother taking me to a certain neighborhood, near the beautiful lake I mentioned earlier, and telling me, "You're sure to get people to buy cookies here in Snob Hollow." That was her term for the wealthiest section of the downtown community. I grew up convinced that having money meant looking down on others and thinking you were better than they were.

Because I thought it was terrible to have money and look down on others, I did a good job of making sure I never had any money to speak of. It honestly didn't occur to me until I was in my late thirties, while taking a class on Christian principles for money, that if I had money, I would have a means of helping more people. That may seem like the silliest thing I've written so far, but it's true. I thought rich people were unforgivably snooty and judgmental, and I was never going to be one of them.

Yet that didn't take away the longing in my heart, put there by God, to have a space I could appreciate being in. *Nice* doesn't have to mean expensive. Beauty is what it is to you. I have a lovely office with virtually every piece of furniture saved from the scrap heap. What you appreciate grows by leaps and bounds when you take the time to be appreciative.

Don't think that trying to have beauty in your life somehow means you're pretending to be someone you're not. Beauty is essential.

Back to food. Aside from taking what time you can to make the meal enjoyable, nutrition is vitally important to healing your brain and body.

Rainbows are beautiful, and they're the best way to ensure good nutrition. By that, I mean we should aim for different colored fruits and vegetables. Look at the colors of the rainbow – red, orange, yellow, green, blue, indigo, and violet (let's combine those last two and call it purple). Think about what foods of each color you might enjoy. Different colored foods give us the different kinds of nutrition we need to heal.

As much nutrition as there may be in Brussels sprouts, if

you hate them, don't force it. You have some free time now, time that you used to spend on your addiction. Use it to find recipes, try different foods as you can afford them, and figure out healthy meals that you're grateful to have. (Did you know, for instance, that Brussels sprouts taste quite different if instead of boiling or steaming them, you slice them thinly and add them to a stir-fry or pan-fry them? Especially if you add a bit of diced bacon and a sprinkle of chopped nuts.)

Your brain and body need good nutrition to heal. Getting out from under the grip of addiction is a healing process, and you can't heal very well on a pot of coffee and a dozen donuts. I'm sorry. Truly. Life would be easier for so many of us if only that weren't true.

The ultimate goal in recovery is two-fold: first, healing your brain, and second, turning your thoughts and actions towards the life God intended you to live. Healing requires rest, good nutrition, exercise, and companionship. The food you eat is one aspect of giving your body the raw materials it needs to carry out essential repairs. *So, whether you eat or drink, or whatever you do, do all to the glory of God* (1 Corinthians 10:31).

Whole foods, foods that are close to their natural state, are more expensive, yes. They're also more filling. What you lose in quantity, you make up for in quality. If you've had a drinking problem, you may crave sweet things because there's a lot of sugar in alcohol. One way to reduce the craving for sweets is to consume something crunchy, raw, and sweet – like apples and carrots. These will provide nutrition and help keep sugar cravings at bay. Please don't go for replacement sugar via diet sodas. They're terrible for you. (As are sugary sodas.)

Everyone who knows me knows I'm a huge advocate for drinking water. Water helps flush you out. If you're not drinking water, your cells are sitting in their own little individual waste puddles. Yuck. Drink water. Learn to love it. Dress it up a bit, if you like, with a dash of concentrated lemon or lime juice. Don't do (and I'm laughing as I write this) what some of my loved ones do and tell me, "I don't like water!"

After fruits and vegetables, eat protein. There are many ways to cook decent amounts of real chicken, beef, fish, turkey, and other meat. And don't forget beans and nuts, which are sources of protein too. The key is to find what works for you and keep the goal in mind. The goal is to heal your body and brain by giving your body the best variety of healthy foods you can.

If the only things you can afford are off-brand frozen vegetables, so be it. Spend another dollar for a shaker of dried parsley for color. Go easy on the salt. Just look for little ways you can increase the nutrition and attractiveness of your food, understanding every little step counts towards healing your body and brain.

Note – every little step counts. One of the sneaky ways the addicted brain lures you into indulging in addiction again is by saying, "Just today. Just relax for one day, that's all. If you do it today and not tomorrow, then you'll be all right. One day off won't hurt you." The addicted brain suggests the little steps you've made towards recovery are so tiny as to be worthless, and if you indulge today, no problem, you just do without tomorrow. You must reverse that thought process. Today matters. Today is it! You're not guaranteed to have a tomorrow. Your loved ones aren't guaranteed to be around tomorrow. What you do today absolutely matters, and don't let your addicted brain suggest otherwise. I've worked with people who lost years of their lives to this crazy, cunning lie.

And last but most important – pray. Pray for wisdom on what foods to choose and how to spend what money you have on providing the best nutrition for yourself – and your family if you have responsibilities for others.

God answers prayer. James 1:5 says, *If any of you lacks*

wisdom, let him ask God, who gives generously to all without reproach, and it will be given him. He also says to ask without doubting (James 1:6). Believe God will give you the wisdom you need to live life according to his design. If you're asking God for wisdom on how to go about eating well to heal, he's not going to suggest you're silly for not already knowing. That's what it means when it says God gives wisdom generously to all who ask without reproach. It means just go ahead and ask. Ask again if you've forgotten the answer. Ask once more if you're not sure you understood the answer. Ask yet again if you thought you understood but now you're confused.

At no point is this process is the Good Lord going to say, "I've already told you a hundred times. Now stop asking!" Our heavenly Father knows our heart, and he wants us to seek him in all our ways *and he rewards those who seek him* (Hebrews 11:6). He told Jeremiah to *seek me and find me, when you seek me with all your heart* (Jeremiah 29:13). We must not try to

> Maybe God has answers I never imagined.

depend on our own understanding just because we think we ought to know the answer already. Proverbs 3:5-6 tells us to *trust in the LORD with all your heart, and do not lean on your own understanding. In all your ways acknowledge him, and he will make straight your paths.*

I know there've been times in my life when I've hesitated to pray for something. There was a time when I desperately wanted to lose weight, for instance, but I wasn't praying about it. I figured I knew the answer. You just have to exercise (groan) and eat right (salads with awful diet dressing night after night). So why pray?

Why pray when I know the answer? Because, maybe, just maybe, I don't know *all* the answers. Maybe God loves us enough to want to delight and surprise us – kind of like the way we want to delight and surprise those we love. Maybe God has answers I never imagined. Of course he does! He's God. He wants to give us good gifts, *if you then, who are evil, know how to give good gifts to your children, how much more will your Father who is in heaven give good things to those who ask him!* (Matthew 7:11). These are even more than we could ask for or imagine, for he *is able to do far more abundantly than all that we ask or think, according to the power at work within us* (Ephesians 3:20). When we pray and he gives, then we give him the glory and others see our God is a living God (Acts 14:15).

Pray. Pray all the time. Pray about EVERYTHING. Cast *all your anxieties on him, because He cares for you* (1 Peter 5:7). *Rejoice always, pray without ceasing, give thanks in all circumstances; for this is the will of God in Christ Jesus for you* (1 Thessalonians 5:16-18).

If you don't have a lot of money for food, or if your struggle is with an eating disorder, or if there are other food issues – pray about them. God gives wisdom about things we need to know about, and he gives it generously. Repeatedly. Without ever suggesting we're silly for not already knowing the answer.

Chapter 7

Taking a Walk

If you're trying to make changes in your life, then you're trying to do something new. Exercise (making sure your doctor okays it first, of course) is not only good for the body, it's good for the mind, and it increases your brain's capability for neurogenesis.[8]

What's that?

Exercise increases your brain's ability to form new neural networks. Why do you need new neural networks? Because you're trying to learn a new way to live life. You need your brain to be in top shape for learning. You have to give your brain new material to work with.

You know that rigid, narrow thought-process problem we were talking about? Your addicted brain has well-formed neural networks. There are things in your brain that just go together now. Automatically. At this point, you literally can't even imagine one without the other. And if your brain doesn't have

---

8   Carl Ernst et al., "Antidepressant Effects of Exercise: Evidence for an Adult-Neurogenesis Hypothesis?" *Journal of Psychiatry & Neuroscience* 31, no. 2 (March 2006): 84-92.

new material to work with, new material to form new neural networks with, you'll struggle to do life differently.

If you look at a convenience store and think smokes and a forty-ounce, or if you walk into a grocery store and head for the beer aisle, or if you think about going to the doctor's office and start getting cold sweats because that's where you got your pain meds, or if you see a needle or a lighter or a copper sink scrubber and suddenly your heart's in your throat – your brain has very, very well-established neural networks that need to be replaced with new and good habits, new neural networks. And that requires new material, which is where exercise comes in.

I'm going to suggest to you that the best form of exercise you can do is walking. That's because being in a hurry, rushing, feeling stressed, and trying to get to the gym to pound out an exercise routine aren't very helpful in the short term. Right now, you need to send the message to your brain that you have time. Plenty of time. You in fact have all the time in the world you need for what you need to do and for what God has planned for you, because it's all his time anyway.

You need to not be stressed, not feel stressed, not give in to stress, not allow stress to run rampant or sit on you like an anxious ticking clock, because stress will drive your brain to suggest that if you use or indulge, you'll feel better. Stress will drive you to think and feel as though you can't handle it, whatever "it" may be, and that you might as well quit fooling yourself into thinking you can.

Stress = thoughts of using.
Exercise = the ability to think new thoughts.
Walking = exercise that isn't adding stress.

The way your brain gets the message that you're not stressed, and in fact have all the time in the world, is by you slowing down, going for a walk, taking in beauty, and not rushing around like someone who's trying to pack the rest of his life into the next twenty-four hours.

You can use your body and your behavior to convey the specific message to your brain that you want your brain to have. If you take deep breaths and move slowly, when in fact you want to rush around because you're on the edge of panic, you won't really fool your brain. It'll feel the stress anyway and send you messages like "Come on!" "Hurry up!" "This is taking forever!"

Interestingly, though, if you continue to take deep breaths and move at a deliberate pace, your brain will soon cooperate.

There's nothing good that's going to come from rushing around and being stressed.

We've established that your body and brain are connected, so now you need to use that connection for your benefit instead of being ruled by it. You need to use your body to send the message to your brain to relax and calm down, instead of allowing your brain to send the message to your body that it's time to freak out.

The addicted brain is under constant stress because life interferes with addiction. The addicted brain wants to get everything out of the way as quickly as possible to maximize the amount of time available to enjoy the addiction.

You must undo that message. There's nothing good that's going to come from rushing around and being stressed, and you've got to make sure your brain understands that.

My mother had a plaque on the wall in the kitchen of our home that said, "The hurrier I go, the behinder I get." When I find myself getting ramped up because I'm on the verge of running late, and I feel my heart start to beat faster and my thoughts begin to race, I think of that saying and take a deep breath and force myself to consider what's truly necessary in this moment?

Not rushing means not speeding while driving or texting while driving. It means not trying to multi-task, especially since we know people grossly overestimate their abilities in multi-tasking. Studies have shown that multi-tasking generally results in two or more activities being done simultaneously but poorly. It would be better to do one activity at a time and do it well. If that activity is supposed to be spending quality time with someone else, multi-tasking should not be an option.[9]

What we're discussing now is the early stages of trying to turn away from addiction. Retraining your brain to accept that you're not stressed and not in a hurry means not rushing around. However, the positive effects of exercise on the brain are greater if the exercise is moderate.[10] So if you can, under your doctor's supervision, implement a moderate exercise program. With safe, moderate exercise, you'll experience better brain effects.

Be careful though. Many persons with an addiction have a pervasive sense of "If one is good, two must be better." "If a half-hour is good, three hours must be better." Resist these thought patterns in all areas. Walking at a moderate pace and breathing at a moderate rate, while maintaining a positive attitude for as much time as you can spare without feeling stressed, injuring yourself, or failing to manage your time well, is perfect. Nothing more is needed to begin with. Further, if you're praying for wisdom in all areas, you can certainly pray for wisdom regarding increasing your exercise level if and when it seems appropriate.

---

9   Eyal Ophir, Clifford Nass, and Anthony D. Wagner, "Cognitive control in media multitaskers," *Proceedings of the National Academy of Sciences of the United States of America* 106, no. 37 (2009): 15583-15587; published ahead of print August 24, 2009, doi:10.1073/pnas.0903620106.

10   Kai Diederich et al., "Effects of Different Exercise Strategies and Intensities on Memory Performance and Neurogenesis," *Frontiers in Behavioral Neuroscience* 11 (16 March 2017): doi:10.3389/fnbeh.2017.00047.

Chapter 8

Coping with Stress

This is not a how-to on eliminating stress from your life. I'm going to discuss stress and anxiety later, but meanwhile, this is just a quick word on stress management.

Do it.

Learn how to not feel stressed. Learn how to take deep breaths, re-focus your thoughts, and get your heart rate down.

Learn how to sit quietly, for a minute at a time at first, until you can feel how your body responds when you're completely relaxed and completely sober. This will help you establish a baseline, so you recognize when you're becoming stressed. And that, in turn, will allow you to take action sooner.

Why is it important to learn to manage stress?

Because stress increases the desire to indulge in addiction.

Stress also interferes greatly with learning. If you're going to learn a new way of living (joyfully, without addiction), it'll happen a lot faster without the burden of stress.

The essentials of stress management (besides praying and spending time in worship) include nutrition, exercise, a regular schedule that involves as much daylight as possible, rest, and good coping skills. And when I say coping skills, I'm talking about deep breathing, calming activities, and contact with others who love the Lord and are trustworthy to be around.

Including as much daylight as possible is necessary for most people so that they don't feel as though they've lost the day, but really had the chance to experience and accomplish something during the day. *Light is sweet, and it is pleasant for the eyes to see the sun* (Ecclesiastes 11:7). Many of the people I've known who struggle with addiction have second shift jobs and rarely see much of the light of day. They continue this schedule on their days off, and their isolation grows. They're sleeping while others are working, and they're up late at night while others are sleeping. If the unnatural scheduling of second or third shift is harming you, but you have no other income source, pray that the Lord will bring about a change in your situation.

Getting a good night's sleep is an essential part of stress management. God's Word says, *It is in vain that you rise up early and go late to rest, eating the bread of anxious toil; for he gives to his beloved sleep* (Psalm 127:2). Develop a routine that sends a clear signal to your body and brain that it's time to go to sleep, and don't make your bedroom like a second living room where you read, eat, and watch TV.

One example of the calming activities I mentioned above is making a cup of tea. God made endlessly different kinds of plants, and because he doesn't act on a whim, I have to believe there was a purpose for this. One purpose is tea. There are more than a dozen different kinds of teas labeled as relaxing, but chances are not everyone will find every kind relaxing. There's lemon balm, chamomile, lavender, peppermint, ash-wagandha, catnip, passion flower, linden, valerian, green tea, and even decaffeinated black tea. If you smell the box, you'll have an idea of which tea relaxes you. If you smell the box and straighten up with an "Oooh," that would be a refreshing tea for you. If you smell the box and go "Ahhh," you may have found a good relaxing one. If you can't smell the box because it's wrapped in plastic, go to a specialty food store, do the sniff test, then head back to the regular grocers. Doing the work of recovery takes time and effort.

Again, calming activities result in you sending the message to yourself that now is a time to be calm, not stressed. We use the actions of our bodies to convey the message to our brains that we want our brains to receive. If you're walking in little circles in your living space with racing thoughts of a stressful situation and not engaging in a calming activity, you're allowing your troubled brain to run the show.

If your means of safe escape is to bury yourself in television, please, please pray to be able to leave this behind as much as possible. Television, for the most part, isn't good for you. It's an easy form of escape that erodes your brain's ability to focus and concentrate. This makes it harder to read anything more complicated than a children's book. Television reduces your attention span. If someone is trying to tell you something and doesn't get to the point right away, you'll grow impatient. This is bad for relationships.

Television consumes precious time, and many shows desensitize you to violence, sarcasm, and lust.

Television consumes precious time, and many shows desensitize you to violence, sarcasm, and lust. Being desensitized is common in our culture of complaint and dissatisfaction, but it results in tender feelings being eroded and laughed at, and this damages close relationships. Even documentaries are filmed in a way that casts doubt and suspicion on their subject, not to provide the viewer with objective education but simply to generate sales. Mass media is best taken in tiny doses.

For those of you who thrive on stress:

God says, *Be still, and know that I am God* (Psalm 46:10).

If you're used to lots of stress, then working to eliminate stress may physically feel kind of like being depressed. You might feel bored. You might get restless.

If you're accustomed to living from one crisis to another, I would urge you to pray about why you continue with this. Does it feel good to be needed? Is the adrenaline rush of an emergency exciting? Does it distract you from working on your own life?

Living from one crisis to another interferes greatly with your recovery.

Enjoying beauty and food, taking good exercise through walking, managing our stress, and refusing to rush are foundational things to put in place along with praying and reading your Bible. You can do these things alone. If this were the complete answer, we'd all be living like Thoreau in *Walden Pond*. He found it preferable to be alone. For most of us, however, life involves others.

So what to do about those others?

Chapter 9

Being Humble

St. Augustine said, "It was pride that changed angels into devils; it is humility that makes men as angels."

"If you are humble, nothing will touch you, neither praise nor disgrace, because you know what you are." Mother Teresa of Calcutta

Can you imagine never worrying about whether someone knows you're in recovery? Can you imagine not feeling sad or resentful when you don't get the recognition or the pat on the back you hoped for? This is what Mother Teresa wants us to understand about being humble; it means if someone says, "You were a no-good, lying snake," you can say, "Yes, I was, and there are days when I feel like I still am." It means that if you do all the work for a project and someone else gets all the credit, you can be okay with that, because you know God saw the truth.

What else does it mean to be humble?

It means not feeling compelled to have the last word.

It means not thinking you need to set someone straight when you believe they're wrong about you.

It means not bragging.

It means that when it's not your turn to talk, you keep quiet and let others speak.

What it *doesn't* mean is thinking poorly of yourself, putting yourself down, or being a doormat under someone else's abusive heels. It doesn't mean not standing up for yourself or for others who are being mistreated.

In Philippians 2:3-4, Paul wrote to the church, *Do nothing from selfish ambition or conceit, but in humility count others more significant than yourselves. Let each of you look not only to his own interests, but also to the interests of others.*

If you're unable to trust God, this will never sit comfortably in your heart and mind.

Many people who've developed an addiction have experienced abuse and trauma in the past. You may have experienced a physically or emotionally unsafe environment growing up. Perhaps you were physically punished in extreme and frightening ways for accidents or things you couldn't control. Maybe it was never safe for you to show anger or frustration or to express certain thoughts or feelings.

An environment like this produces a whole host of dysfunctional ways of dealing with life: ways to hide who you are, ways to avoid responsibility if something goes wrong, ways to blame or find fault, ways to avoid certain subjects, ways to resist feeling certain emotions, ways to boast so people know you're not a loser. The list goes on and on and on.

The idea of putting others before yourself or thinking of others first, the basic concept of humility, may be so alien you have no idea how to fit this into any safe way of being in the world. Maybe the idea of putting others first creates a huge well of resentment. No one ever put *you* first. Why should you have to put anyone else first?

I think if we look at a few concrete examples, this will be easier to consider and put into practice.

Think about being in a group of people. Someone tells a story about their very bad day. "I woke up late because the power went out last night and my alarm didn't go off. Then I found the dog had puked in my only good pair of work shoes. My car wouldn't start because the door didn't close all the way last night, and the dome light drained the battery. By the time I got to work, my supervisor was so mad he sent me home without pay; now I'll be fifty bucks short next paycheck and eating ramen noodles all week because I won't have money for groceries."

Human nature often wants to respond in one of the following ways:

Response #1: Tell the person how they ought to live their life differently to avoid this kind of problem.

Don't do it. Even if it's your own child, resist the urge to launch into a speech about how they should put a backup battery in their alarm clock, "or use the alarm on the phone you're on all the time!" Don't tell them to buy the dog a chew toy or put their shoes away. Don't point out that if they made a habit of always locking their car, they'd notice when it didn't lock the night before; they would have realized the door was ajar.

Don't try to fix other people's problems like that.

Don't try to fix other people's problems like that.

When you try to fix someone else's problems, you're saying, "I know how you need to run your life. I'd be better at running your life than you are." That's not true. We have no idea what struggles others face, and it's arrogant to assume that if someone did as we say, their life would be fine.

Further, even if you're fifty years older than the other person and a hundred times wiser than they are, saying "I could do your life better" doesn't encourage anyone, and it feels awful to hear.

Humility says, "Yes, I've had my alarm fail to go off because the power went out before. I got a backup battery for my clock because the last time it happened, the consequences were rough."

Humility shares truthfully and appropriately from the heart with "I" statements. Humility doesn't say, "You know, what you really ought to do is . . ." I can listen to what you did in your own life much more easily than I can listen to you tell me what I should do with mine.

If you read the book of Proverbs, you see King Solomon saying, "My son, listen and take heed. Don't be tempted by sin." This is when you can and should give advice as a parent – before things go wrong. Once someone has messed up, it's time to listen and then share your own experience. If the solution isn't obvious, asking "Do you think there's a way to keep this from happening again?" shows respect for the other person's intelligence as well as a certain amount of sympathy for their plight.

Being humble means not saying "I told you so" in order to get credit for the sage advice you gave earlier.

Many people are familiar with the Bible verses that suggest sparing the rod may spoil the child. *Whoever spares the rod hates his son, but he who loves him is diligent to discipline him* (Proverbs 13:24). *Discipline your son, for there is hope* (Proverbs 19:18), and *do not withhold discipline from a child* (Proverbs 23:13).

Fewer are aware of the Bible verses about not provoking your children to anger as in Ephesians 6:4, which says, *Fathers, do not provoke your children to anger, but bring them up in the discipline and instruction of the Lord.* Colossians 3:21 says, *Fathers, do not provoke your children, lest they become discouraged.* Children are going to mess up. If your response is only to tell them how to fix their life, it may result in their hiding failures and disappointments from you. Everyone makes mistakes. If you're willing to share yours with your children in an age-appropriate manner, it will be a lot easier for them to share themselves.

I participated in an experiment at work once that showed how poorly advice is received. We paired up in groups. I was paired with one of the most helpful men I've ever known. The exercise asked for one person to talk about a goal. In round one, the other person would offer advice. In round two, the other person would ask questions and seek to understand.

I went first, of course. I said I would like to exercise daily, but I always seemed to run out of time. When my co-worker jumped in eagerly and helpfully with great advice, though, I could feel my brain digging in its heels like a little kid. To everything he said, I automatically thought, "No, that won't work" or "Tried that, didn't make a difference."

The exercise showed that when someone gives advice, it doesn't go over well. I knew this was an exercise. I'd already been told I'd be given advice. I expected I would accept the advice from this person I trusted. Nope. My mind went straight to rebellious, teenage thoughts of "You don't understand; that won't work for me!" It was a great exercise.

In round two, when my co-worker asked questions about what I had tried that did or didn't work in a tone of voice that conveyed genuine interest, I was happy to share. Because he had showed himself to be trustworthy in our conversation together, I could honestly consider whether I had put in my best effort.

We're so contrary in our perceptions and reactions sometimes. We go to someone and seek their help, yet when they offer advice, we reject it. I imagine most everyone has had this experience. I've read that in dating and marital relationships, when a woman brings up a problem she's had, the man often wants to fix the problem while the woman only wants him to listen. The man wonders why she's bringing it up if she doesn't want the problem solved; the woman wonders why he can't just listen.

If I tell you all the reasons why I'm not accomplishing something I want to accomplish, chances are you'll want to offer advice and tell me how to achieve my stated goal. If I don't listen, you might conclude either I'm not trying to achieve my goal or I think your advice is no good.

The solution to this mess of poor communication and false assumptions is a humble "I" statement: "Here's something I tried, and it worked well for me."

Resist the urge to try to pin the other person down once you've shared. Don't follow up with "So, do you think that would work for you?" You're not there to give advice. If you try to press them for their response, what you're really doing is seeking recognition for the advice you weren't supposed to be giving in the first place.

During that exercise, when my co-worker asked sincerely, "What have you tried?" I was happy to share the ways I'd tried to solve the problem. I was also happy to share the reasons why I believed the things I'd tried hadn't worked out. In response, he encouraged me to consider what I'd learned from my trial and error. As a result, I finally realized the most likely plan of exercise that I would stick to would involve having an exercise partner. I needed a person to whom I would be accountable. Accountability is a great way to stay committed to change.

If you want to help someone change their ways, be humble. Share things you've tried that worked or didn't work by using "I-statements." Sympathize. Ask them if they've thought about why certain things didn't work. Humbly assume that they have the means to figure it out; if you're a safe sounding board, they might figure it out by talking with you. You help by being honest and sharing about yourself, not by telling someone what to do.

A final note here. Teaching isn't the same thing as giving

advice. If I ask you how to install a dishwasher, it's because I've never installed one, and I hope you will teach me. If you install them for a living, you'll likely have additional advice to give regarding the installation, the tools that will be needed, the amount of time to set aside for the project, and so on. A good gauge of when your requested teaching has crossed the line into advice is when the person you're talking to starts fidgeting. When someone looks as though they'd like to get away, they're no longer listening.

Response #2: One nanosecond after the person finishes their story of their rotten day, you launch into your story of your even worse one.

"Oh, you think that's bad. Last week, my day started . . ." Don't do that. Don't be the person whose story is worse. Especially don't do that every time and without even acknowledging you heard the other person. *Know this, my beloved brothers: Let every person be quick to hear, slow to speak* (James 1:19). This is humility. This is allowing the other person to have the spotlight for a moment and to feel heard.

> **Don't be the person whose story is worse.**

A long time ago, I read that the opposite of love is not hate but indifference. We all want to matter to someone. When we speak, we want to be heard and understood. When you jump in to best someone else, you convey that their story wasn't very impressive or important and yours is better. This is not humility.

Oddly enough, acting this way is a common trait among people who aren't used to being heard. You'd think that people who are used to being treated disrespectfully or being brushed aside themselves would understand how it makes people feel, but in fact, those are the very people who will jump in fast because, in their heart, they feel they might not get another chance.

Often, people with an urgent need to speak are people who

grew up with broken promises from loved ones. Every good thing was expressed as "maybe someday" or "maybe if we get enough time," but no one ever made time. Kids who wanted to share something got brushed aside with a quick "Uh-huh, now go play." These kids are now adults whose speech conveys this fear of going unnoticed, which they still find painful. In their mind, if you don't listen right now, you may never listen.

I participated in another exercise that showed me the depth of my own need to feel heard. It was at a conference about relationships. The facilitator asked us, as usual, to split into groups of two. One person would tell a story, the other person would listen. Guess who offered to tell a story? Yes, me! We were to aim for a three-minute story. During minute one, the listener was to listen attentively. During minute two, the listener was to go into "freeze" mode – head down, no eye contact, no movement, no sign of hearing. Minute three, the listener would again resume listening attentively.

It was terrible. Minute two, when my listener put his head down, I wanted to stop my story. I even leaned towards him to try to re-engage him at first, before I realized what I was doing. I had to force myself to sit up straight and continue. Losing his attention made me very unhappy. Even before I started speaking, I was kind of put off because I think he thought I was attracted to him. I wasn't, but when the facilitator said, "Pair up," I immediately asked him if he wanted to be my partner. If you've ever had the experience of being the odd one out, you know how awkward it feels to be without a partner. I didn't want to be in that position, so I jumped at the first opportunity to snag someone.

So here I am talking to someone I think may not even like me very much, and when he puts his head down, I'm all "Oh no! Hey! Come back!" and have to restrain myself. One minute I'm telling my story to an attentive if somewhat uncomfortable listener, the next he's asleep with his eyes open, and I feel huge anxiety. I continue, but I'm talking to someone who's not listening and it doesn't feel good. It feels a bit ridiculous. I know he can still hear me, but it doesn't matter one bit.

Minute three, he springs back up and my heart soars. I'm so grateful to have regained the attention of this person even though, except for listening attentively, he hasn't been warm or friendly towards me at all. This was an extremely effective exercise to show how much we treasure undivided attention from a person, almost any person.

By the way, if you read this and think that it's probably just me, probably just the way I am, and you don't think it would bother you, I suggest you give it a try. In fact, I insist. Okay, I'm in no position to insist, but in *Alcoholics Anonymous* it says, "contempt prior to investigation" is a very bad thing.[11] If you shrug off a good idea that's worked for others just because you find it silly, what's that about? If you haven't tried, then you don't really know.

If you jump in to speak the second someone is done speaking or even interrupt before they're done, you're stealing their joy. We all want to be heard, to be understood, to believe we matter. Willingness to hear and understand and respect is conveyed in patient listening, not jumping in to cut the other person off and focus attention back on ourselves.

Be the humble person who trusts God and knows he sees you keep yourself in check. Know that God sees your love in not jumping in to steal another person's moment. This is being humble.

Response #3: Maybe you don't roll your eyes, but you hear a story of someone's rotten day, and you think, "What a loser."

---

11   "Spiritual Experience," Appendix 2, *Alcoholics Anonymous: The Story of How Many Thousands of Men and Women Have Recovered from Alcoholism,* 4th ed. (New York: Alcoholics Anonymous World Services, Inc., 2001), 568.

Humility recognizes people share for all kinds of reasons and even unbelievable stories have a purpose. Humility allows you to see this is a person who perhaps doesn't have a more interesting or more plausible story to tell. Maybe they're very preoccupied with the money they lost by being sent home. Maybe this person isn't joking about the ramen noodles and hasn't been eating properly even on their regular income. Maybe they're worried they're going to lose their job. Or maybe this person is lying through their teeth, and you feel it with every fiber of your being, and you want to call them on it.

Humility is showing the love of Jesus Christ by simply saying, "Wow, sounds rough." If that's all you can manage to say, say it. If you're thinking terrible things about this person, pray in silence for forgiveness. Keep in mind this person is loved and wanted by the Lord Jesus. If you give opportunity to terrible thoughts, this will come across in your body language. The other person may not know the details of your thoughts, but they will feel the tone of your emotion towards them.

Being humble means not allowing yourself to entertain the kind of vicious, spiteful, or judgmental thoughts that arise when you hear someone else describing something you believe is foolish or even untrue.

Why be humble, though? Does it actually impact addiction?

Addiction involves a loss of control. Being humble is being self-controlled. Addiction is allowing the pleasure-seeking, sinful nature of the flesh to take over and be selfish, self-absorbed, and self-centered. Being humble is trusting God sees all and understanding your loving patience is a balm to someone else's soul – even if it doesn't seem like it in the moment.

When you practice behaviors in opposition to addiction, you give your body and brain the opportunity to learn what it feels like to not be ruled by passion, pleasure, or avoidance of pain. You give your body and brain the experience of being self-possessed, dignified, and admirable in how you handle things. When you practice being humble, you practice a form of not yielding to self-gratification. Addiction is rushing into instant gratification. Humility is denying it.

If you hear a story and want to quickly jump in and tell a better one, that's immediate gratification of the desire for attention, and it is not humble. If you hear how someone has messed up and you want to immediately jump in and tell them how to fix their problem, that's a prideful assumption of having answers they lack. If someone else's consistent failures make you laugh or joke or roll your eyes, you're taking a perverse delight in their misfortune because it makes you feel better about your own.

> Being humble slows things down and takes others' needs into consideration.

There is a patience to humility. There is love. There is the ability to pause and consider another human being as worthy. Being humble slows things down and takes others' needs into consideration.

WARNING! DANGER!

Many confuse the idea of being humble with being a door-mat. "I humble myself and let my sister talk trash about me," or "I'm trying to be humble so I never say anything when my wife makes jokes at my expense." Perhaps you're a supervisor at work, and you've recently heard a little bit about leading with a servant heart. Now, you think being humble means not saying anything when someone undermines your authority – be it an employee or your superior.

Not true. Being humble is not suggesting you let all conflicts go. In fact, it would be a gross misunderstanding if you take the idea of being humble as a suggestion to avoid conflict. In

Jesus's first sermon, he said, *Blessed are the peacemakers, for they shall be called sons of God* (Matthew 5:9). You can't very well be a peacemaker if you avoid conflict.

There are things, many things, we ought to let roll off our back, but there are times when the right thing is to speak up. *He has told you, O man, what is good: and what does the Lord require of you but to do justice, and to love kindness, and to walk humbly with your God?* (Micah 6:8). Doing justice is never accomplished by avoiding conflict; it's achieved by learning the humility and self-control required to be a peacemaker.

Before moving on to other people's issues, we need to address the fact that there isn't a set list of rules we can follow and pat ourselves on the back for sticking to. *So whoever knows the right thing to do and fails to do it, for him it is sin* (James 4:17). *Thus, sinning against your brothers and wounding their conscience when it is weak* is a sin against Jesus Christ (1 Corinthians 8:12). *For it is God who works in you, both to will and to work for his good pleasure* (Philippians 2:13).

Bottom line? You'll have to pray about which conflicts you should let slide and which ones call for you to do justice and work out a peaceful resolution with gracious humility. The only way to know what God is calling you to do is to maintain a daily, constant relationship with him. We accomplish this through Bible reading, prayer, and fellowship with other believers who also engage in daily Bible reading and prayer. Then you'll experience the truth in Jesus's saying, *My sheep hear my voice, and I know them, and they follow me* (John 10:27). You'll learn what is and isn't good for you personally, because of the unique way you're made. You'll learn to know when the Holy Spirit is nudging you to speak and when you ought to stay quiet.

If all you had to do was follow the rules, you wouldn't need to pray. You wouldn't need constant contact with God. You wouldn't need to listen for the voice of Jesus expressed through the Holy Spirit, because you'd already know what to do. And if you always knew what to do, you'd be a self-righteous know-it-all.

God has designed us to be in close relationship with him, in part so we don't turn into a bunch of over-bearing, over-confident rule-followers. There was a group like this in the Bible. They were called Pharisees. Jesus called them hypocrites. Repeatedly. Read about them in Matthew chapter 23.

Jesus said that in their insistence on following the rules that they expanded beyond what God had originally said to do, the Pharisees shut the door of heaven in people's faces (Matthew 23:13). Matthew 12:7 describes how Jesus (quoting Hosea 6:6) said the Pharisees wouldn't have become the condemnatory, rule-following hypocrites they undoubtedly were if they had understood God desires mercy rather than sacrifice.

God desires our love and our individual obedience to him. To know how to carry out his design for our lives requires that we read the Bible and pray. We can't just follow the rules or blindly assume good works are sufficient for accomplishing his purposes in our lives. God's ways are not our ways.

Chapter 10

Communicating Well

In talking about humility, I mentioned communicating
appropriately from the heart with I-statements. When I
facilitate group discussions, the one thing I say that's most
irritating to the group is, "Please use I-statements." I know it
exasperates them, but I say it anyway, because the difference
it makes is huge.

An I-statement is personal testimony, which is powerful.
Using I-statements feels more personal and vulnerable, which
is why it's more powerful. It's also why people shy away from
using them. But you-statements make assumptions that get
in the way of your message and don't carry the same weight.

For example:

> "When I get up in the morning now, I like to spend
> a few minutes reading a devotional while I enjoy my
> first cup of coffee. It's amazing what a difference a
> few minutes has made in my day. I used to wake up
> grumpy and rush out the door. I don't think I ever
> felt good until after noon when I did that!"

If I said that to a group about myself, there's no room for argument. You can't reasonably tell me my day isn't better for starting out in this manner. You might then discuss what you do in the morning, and we can compare. We can have a nice conversation about our morning routines.

Now suppose someone in a group starts out:

> "You know how in the morning you get a cup of coffee and then . . ."

> "Nah, I don't drink coffee."

> "Hah! I work second shift; I'm never up in the morning!"

> "Well, you know when you're getting ready to start your day, if you read a devotional . . ."

> "I don't have time for that!"

> "I can't find time to make coffee, forget about sitting and reading."

> "What I'm saying is, just for me it makes a difference."

> "Well, that's you."

If you make assumptions with you-statements, you risk people disagreeing with what you claim also applies to them. This is why I couch so many of my statements in terms like *often* or *frequently* or *a lot of people*. This is known as softening my speech. Soft speech invites conversation and sharing, whereas hard speech invites argument.

Hard speech would be saying, for example, "The best pet is a small dog." If I said that in a group, there would be a clamor as some felt it necessary to tell me how wrong I was. If I said, "I believe the best pet is a small dog," that's a little better. If

I said, "I believe the best pet for me is a small dog," I invite a question or the sharing of a difference. You might ask why I believe the best pet for me is a small dog. Or you might say, "I like cats." Flat, hard statements invite argument. An argument doesn't mean yelling and shouting; it means expressing a different point of view. Add the emotion of anger, however, and the argument may turn into yelling and shouting.

The point is that when you share details that are clearly about yourself and not the world in general, you invite people to get to know you better or to share about themselves. This is the basis for forming a relationship. Flat, hard statements form an argument not a relationship.

> How you speak matters – always.

Tell your own story with I-statements. Let your own light shine. It really does make a huge difference.

Before we talk any more about talking, please know that I know it's not fun to guard your speech. Sometimes it can be very tiring, especially with people who are easily offended. Sometimes we justify poor speech: "I try to be nice, but . . .," "Sometimes things just need to be said," or "I know I shouldn't have said it, but I was so angry!"

You have a decision to make.

Is your goal to communicate – actually convey information to someone – or is it to hear the sound of your own voice? Worse, is it your goal to take shots at someone?

Do you want to be understood, or do you want to be dismissed?

Do you want others to listen, or do you want them to try to get away?

How you speak matters – always.

What does communication have to do with addiction?

James 3:2 says, *For we all stumble in many ways. And if*

anyone does not stumble in what he says, he is a perfect man, able also to bridle his whole body.

If you could speak perfectly at all times, you'd have control over (the ability to *bridle*) your whole body. I can only imagine!

Death and life are in the power of the tongue (Proverbs 18:21). There are many, many verses in Scripture about the power of words, about speech, about lying tongues and false tongues and unholy chatter. Understanding that death and life are in the power of the tongue sums it up pretty well.

If your addiction is killing you or putting loved ones at risk, you may *urgently* need to put things in place that lead to a life worth staying sober for. You need a life that is enriching, purposeful, joyful, and Spirit-filled. To travel the path to joy where others are involved, you'll need to use the kind of speech God intended.

If you aren't speaking as God intended, then you may be driving away those who love you most. God designed us for relationship with him and with others. How you speak affects the quality of this relationship. Always.

So how to speak?

> *Let your speech always be gracious, seasoned with salt, so that you may know how you ought to answer each person* (Colossians 4:6). *Let no corrupting talk come out of your mouths, but only such as is good for building up, as fits the occasion, that it may give grace to those who hear* (Ephesians 4:29). *A soft answer turns away wrath, but a harsh word stirs up anger* (Proverbs 15:1).

We talked earlier about how you can be humble, speak humbly, and still speak with power, especially in testimony. There's no power in losing your self-control, no power in shouting, cursing, raising your voice, or committing acts of violence; there's only intimidation and fear.

I don't know about you, but when I have "lost it" to greater and lesser degrees, I find myself revisiting the situation in my mind. I think about what the other person said or did; I think about what I said or did. Often, I think of all the ways in which I had *every right*! I had every right to shout or interrupt, every right to be angry and show it!

Then the Holy Spirit goes to work, and after a while, I think a little more on what the other person said. I think about the look on their face as I was letting loose. I think about how it feels to have been so hateful and ugly.

Then I get brave and think about how I could have handled it differently. If it's a stranger, I pray the Lord will forgive me and give grace to that person. If it's a loved one, I can't wait to apologize. I can't wait to speak words that I know, really know, will touch their heart because I know I was wrong. I know that while I may have had reason to be angry, that's no justification for coming unglued.

I know that I can speak with power and still be humble and that I always feel better for doing so. I feel a thousand times better when I speak honestly from the heart and say, "I'm disappointed. I thought we agreed you were going to . . ." rather than yelling, "What the heck? What is wrong with you?"

When I maintain self-control, I feel in control. I feel good when I let the Holy Spirit guide my words, because God is never wrong. I'm the one who's wrong.

Another form of speech that drives people away is speech intended to control another. Some people with addictions have to hustle a lot. Some addictions require a person to hustle for money or rides or food or second chances or a place to stay or the use of a phone.

Have you had someone ask for a ride to the grocery store?

And once they're in the car, they ask, "Could we also stop at the drug store? Oh, and if you wouldn't mind, I'd like to just run in to this other place." This is hustling. It's not as though the person who does this forgot all the places they'd like to go and only remembered them when they got in your car. They know. They also know if they ask up front, the answer will be no.

The speech and behavior that goes with this kind of hustling doesn't disappear in recovery. Neural networks are firmly established in addiction – rigid thought processes; remember? A person with an addiction will look at something they want and think, "Who do I need to persuade? How do I persuade them?" That has become the default setting I refer to as hustling. "How do I get what I want?" There's no prayer or attempt to seek God's will in this behavior.

Hustlers claim the other person can say no, but they purposely choose to ask favors from people who are soft-hearted and tend to say yes.

A while ago, I read about an experiment where troubled teenagers were divided into two groups. Each person in one group was given a tennis ball, and each person in the other group was told to try to get the ball from the person across from them. Not one person in the second group tried asking for the ball. Each tried to physically take it. They didn't ask because they expected the answer would be no. The inability to deal with no leads to controlling behavior.

Honest and brave people just ask, knowing the answer might be no, and trust God with how it works out.

Refusing to allow the possibility of no, or being unable to bear the idea of no, results in speech and behavior that attempts to control, to hustle, and to manipulate.

Controlling speech and behavior is not speech designed to *give grace to those who hear.* Controlling speech is not relational speech. Controlling speech says, "I want what I want, and I want you to give it to me whether you want to or not."

Don't kid yourself. The people around you may not have the words to describe the way controlling speech and behavior is affecting them, but they will resent it. And they will resent you for it. They may say yes because they want to avoid a scene, don't want to make you unhappy, or for any number of reasons they're unable to say no very easily. That doesn't mean your relationship isn't damaged by your use of controlling behavior designed to get your own way.

If you don't speak with the goal of giving grace to those who hear, then what is your goal?

If you want a life that's not filled with hustling, controlling, and manipulating, then you must speak graciously and humbly, and be prepared to hear "no".

Even if your addiction isn't to drugs or alcohol, there's some way you've sought time alone to indulge. If you have friends or family, you must have engaged in behavior to set them aside in order to pursue your addiction. This, too, was hustling behavior. You convinced someone you didn't feel well, or were too busy, or had too much on your mind perhaps. There has certainly been some behavior designed to keep those who love you, or would love you if you let them, at arm's length, so you could pursue your addiction. Sometimes, it's simple intimidation. "Leave me alone!"

> Hustling behaviors will continue in recovery if you don't learn to speak the truth in love.

Fighting an addiction requires an intent to speak the truth in love always and to speak to be heard (Ephesians 4:15).

Hustling behaviors will continue in recovery if you don't learn to speak the truth in love.

Why?

Because these are the behaviors you've used many times

before. They have enabled you to indulge in self-centered, self-ish acts, and that desire doesn't disappear just because you're in recovery. The behaviors that are capable of keeping others at arm's length are well established, and unless you learn to speak the truth in love, those behaviors will continue because they worked.

Most people don't tell their loved ones, "I'm not going to dinner with you tonight because I want to stay home and look at pornography." They don't say, "I don't have the money I owe you because I spent $350 on crack last weekend," or "I can't see you right now because I just ate an entire carton of cookie dough ice cream, and I'm sick."

So when future occasions arise involving situations you'd just as soon not participate in, you've already got a whole host of untruthful or controlling or intimidating patterns of behavior in place. A friend says, "Oh, Jenna's in town; she wants us to go out with her and her husband!" You might think, "Great. They're a lovely couple. I'm looking forward to it." On the other hand, you might think, "Oh no. That woman's voice gets under my skin, and her husband only talks about our country going down the tubes."

If you haven't practiced speaking the truth in love, the imme-diate temptation will be to engage in hustling behavior to avoid dinner with Jenna and her husband. "Well, you know, I've got a lot scheduled this week. You always enjoy them more than I do; you should go without me. Unfortunately, this is really bad timing. Besides, you know I'm not very good at socializing."

This is the start of trying to get out of going without being honest. This is hoping your friend doesn't notice you just don't want to go to dinner with these people. This is hustling. You're trying to manipulate the situation. You want to look good with-out being honest and without giving your friend any chance for further input or allowing further discussion.

Now, speaking the truth in love doesn't mean that when you don't want to go to dinner, you call up Jenna right away and tell her, "I can hardly bear to be in the same room with you people!" That may be speaking the truth, but it's not very loving.

Speaking the truth in love means you should consider your friend's interests and your own. Consider telling your friend, "I know this means a lot to you, and Jenna is great. You know how political her husband is though. I want to try to figure out how to make the best of it." Together, you work out a plan. It may be a plan that limits the time for dinner, or you may arrange for dinner to take place where there's other entertainment.

As much as possible, instead of saying "I know you feel this way, *but* I feel differently," rearrange your words to say, "I know you feel this way, *and* I feel another way." Changing *but* to *and* allows two points of view without pitting them against each other.

I know this may seem very small and very particular. I've heard people say it feels fake to change speech around. Well, yes. If *fake* means not just saying whatever words come to mind, then yeah, it'll feel fake. Yet, intentionally shifting your words around doesn't make them less real or less true. To communicate, we have words and we have body language. If you're considering another person's interests, you have to convey that's what you're doing. You have to choose whether to believe their interests are directly opposed to yours. If so, the word *but* comes in. If there's a workable solution, however, *and* expresses this belief. You can say, "I want this *but* you want that," suggesting you believe there's a conflict. Or you can say, "I want this *and* you want that," suggesting there's work to be done between the two of you.

When you suggest by your tone of voice and your choice of words that there's a solution, you open the door to discussion and greater communication. This is also how words convey care and concern. When you suggest you want to work *with* someone instead of against them, you show them you value their thoughts and feelings about a subject.

Words and body language are the only options we have for communicating in the moment, and body language is more difficult to control than word choice. Words chosen with care reflect care for the person you're speaking to.

But wait! Suppose you use your best words to suggest to your friend a way to have dinner that makes both of you happy, but your friend is annoyed anyway. Maybe your friend thinks you should have been wildly excited about going to dinner with Jenna and her husband in the first place. Here is where dysfunction shows up.

It's dysfunctional to try to control how other people feel. It's wrong. It's also useless. Even if you convince someone to do as you say, you haven't changed how they feel about it. Feelings don't change by force, they change by understanding. In our example, if your friend is annoyed because you weren't excited about something that excited her, then she doesn't understand what the situation feels like for you. When you understand, you have empathy. Maybe you don't feel the same way the other person does, but you get it. When you're just annoyed, however, there's no understanding.

I would never want someone to tell me how to feel about something. I wouldn't want someone to tell me my feelings are wrong. I'm happy to have a discussion regarding my thoughts on virtually any subject. If you tell me my feelings are wrong, though, you tell me my reaction, over which I have no control, is wrong. Basically, I'm wrong in the way I am.

This is a critical point. Our feelings are the product of our experiences and our thoughts. We don't control our feelings. We control our actions, and we control our thoughts with diligent practice. The Bible says in Ephesians 4:26, *Be angry and do not sin; do not let the sun go down on your anger.* The Bible also tells us that certain emotions are harmful, such as envy, which *makes the bones rot* (Proverbs 14:30). Envy, like other emotions, is fueled by our thoughts, which we have to practice controlling. We can control thoughts and behaviors with practice, but not emotions. Our emotions change when our thoughts and behaviors change.

Yet in most families, there's a lot of dysfunctional speech that's intended to control emotions. The speech revolves around trying to direct and control other people's feelings. Family members lay on the guilt when someone doesn't respond as desired. This is often where hustling is established. Within our "families of origin" (a term for the people you grew up with), we may learn

> Our emotions change when our thoughts and behaviors change.

it's not safe to be honest. In a lot of families, if you show your disappointment, you'll be mocked. If you show your anger, you'll be criticized. If you show you're afraid, you'll be laughed at.

Attempts to control feelings happen in big and small ways. Some years ago, when I was already an adult living away from home, my mother tried to convince me I'd be very happy if she sent me a blue-goose wall hanging that was all the rage in kitchen décor. Um, no. "Mom, I don't want a blue goose hanging on my wall." She informed me that I had plenty of wall space, and she was sending it anyway. I was so annoyed!

But I have to admit I've been guilty of the same thing. I recently tried to convince my daughter she should be very grateful for a free pair of sparkly flip-flops. She was perfectly happy with the shoes she had, and besides, she doesn't care for sparkles. If we trust God to provide, we don't have to hang on to useless, excess junk. That's a whole other story though. The point is we want others to feel about things the same way we feel, but often they just don't. And it's okay they don't. It's not a critical issue.

I've heard families when they're shopping for school clothes. "Honey, what do you think of this shirt?" "I don't like it." "Well, you know what? This is the third shirt you haven't liked. As far as I'm concerned, you can just do without new school clothes!"

Um, where did that come from? You're giving your child a choice between lying and accepting something unwanted, or losing out for being honest? That's a lousy choice. And it will get worse if the child takes the shirt and never wears it. You know people do that. They insist on "gifting" you with something you don't want and then wonder what happened to the gift they gave you. Why isn't it being used or worn or displayed? That is controlling.

Dysfunction, of course, gets worse. The phrase "passive-aggressive" gets tossed around a lot, and it's firmly established behavior in dysfunctional families who don't value and prioritize honesty. Understanding what being passive-aggressive looks like and feels like can help correct dysfunctional patterns of family communication.

Most people think of passive-aggressive behavior as giving someone the silent treatment, pouting, and making little sarcastic comments, then denying there was any genuine feeling behind it. These are surface behaviors I know well. In the past, I never wanted to have a conversation with someone when I was angry. I was a big fan of the silent treatment combined with a clenched jaw and pointed stares. However, the underlying message is much more aggressive than we own up to. If you're refusing to speak to someone because you're angry, the underlying message is that person is contemptible to you. They don't deserve you. They don't deserve to know why you're angry or at the very least, not yet. They need to suffer a little first. Wanting someone to suffer emotionally is an act of aggression.

If you cannot talk because you're so angry that you're afraid of saying something hurtful that you cannot take back, then you can at least say that. You can tell someone, "This has me really upset. I'd like to discuss it later, when I'm calmer." That shows love and care and humanity. You should then be the one to reintroduce the subject later, when you're calmed down, knowing it does need to be discussed.

Wanting someone to suffer first shows a lack of respect. Whether we *feel* respect for someone is not the issue – we always need to *demonstrate* respect to others.

My favorite example is when a wife asks her husband what he'd like for dinner. He says, "How about you grill us a couple of steaks?" She's immediately irritated. She thinks, "He knows I don't like using the grill!"

First of all, how much do you keep other people's likes and dislikes in mind? Sometimes, as much as we love someone, we just forget things. They forget things. It happens. Under stress, it happens a lot. Looking forward to the holidays, I baked a cake for my best friend when she came to visit. I like cake. I forgot she doesn't. Oops! Who doesn't like cake, right? See, because I like cake, I think she should, too. The fact that she doesn't is baffling to me. Should I try to tell her how good cake really is and get her to change her mind? No. I apologized and offered to make brownies. She said the pudding poke cake was better than she thought it would be. We moved on. She forgave me for not remembering her dessert preferences.

So (to get back to our story), the wife decides to go ahead and grill the steaks because she thinks, "If I tell him I don't want to, he'll be annoyed, tell me to fix whatever I want, and say I shouldn't have asked him what he wanted in the first place."

Secondly, she makes a choice, but she doesn't see it as a choice. She doesn't acknowledge it as a choice. She's thinking she has to do this or else he'll be annoyed. If you choose a behavior to keep someone else from being annoyed, own up to your choice. You chose peace. You chose their happiness over yours.

Now the grand finale. As she's carrying the steaks out to the grill, one slides off and hits the grass. Picking it up, she says to herself, quite deliberately, "Oh, this one is his."

That is passive-aggressive behavior. It's rude, but it takes place out of sight, under your breath, behind someone's back, or on the sly.

When the husband is eating his steak, he notices a piece of grass and says, "What's this?"

The wife lies, "Oh, that's a new spice; do you like it?" At this point, she's not going to open up and say, "I dropped your steak on the grass and didn't bother to wash it off" because, come on, who wants to own up to such a thing?

Passive-aggressive behavior is a deeply rooted, sad, and sorrowful pattern in too many families. The underlying message is absolutely aggressive, but it may be sugar-coated by sarcasm, or barbed insults and hurtful comments delivered as a "joke."

It is behavior you would clearly recognize as aggressive and hurtful if it happened in front of you, out in the open. If I were carrying two steaks, dropped one, picked it up, and told you the one that fell was yours, you'd think, "Hey! What's that about? You're not even rinsing it off?" You'd be disturbed because you'd rightly see that as poor behavior on my part. You'd be concerned about why I felt no shame. You might even wonder what other things I'd done in secret that you never knew about.

If I said, "I'm not talking to you because I want you to suffer first" it would lose all power. You would likely wonder a lot more about why I wanted you to suffer than you would experience the frustration and concern that I inwardly hoped you would. Calling out the behavior and naming it, taking it from being secret or sly to upfront and obvious, changes everything.

Passive-aggressive behavior ruins relationships because you

allow yourself to think someone else has acted poorly towards you, and therefore they deserve your poor behavior towards them. You won't make it obvious, though, because you want to avoid open conflict. You might even deny having ill feelings if accused, but think to yourself your poor behavior is what they deserve and it serves them right. No. No. No. You can't maintain a loving relationship with thoughts and behavior like this.

You must be the person who can say no, and you must allow your loved ones to say no. If you choose their immediate happiness over your own, do it graciously, consciously, and willingly. If you're doing it because the other person is a tyrant who throws temper tantrums when they don't get their way, pray to move your relationship towards greater love and honesty.

> Have the courage to address conflict openly, directly, and lovingly.

Don't do damage to yourself by justifying passive-aggressive behavior on your part. Be honest and brave. Have the courage to address conflict openly, directly, and lovingly. Good relationships have conflict, but become even stronger and more valuable when that conflict is dealt with.

Another example of dysfunctional communication patterns: I say something snappish that hurts your feelings. Instead of apologizing, I tell you you're too sensitive. Maybe you work up the courage to tell me it makes you feel small or disrespected, and I say with a shrug, "Well, it shouldn't."

There are two important things to keep in mind here. First, if you tell someone their behavior is upsetting, they're bound to be defensive. Proverbs is full of verses about the wise person who is good with being corrected. That's the ideal. The ideal response to being corrected is, "Thank you for pointing that out. I'll work on it." We're not ideal, though, are we? When's the last time you thanked someone for telling you about something you did wrong?

But that's okay. How a person initially responds to your correction isn't nearly as important as the fact that you were willing to address it. Going forward, if I know you'll tell me my lack of kindness was hurtful, sooner or later I'll get tired of hearing about it. I'll be nicer if for no other reason than to not have to listen to you say something about it.

Not long ago, I heard a woman tell a story about her big nose. Now don't get me wrong; she did have a big nose. When she was growing up, her family would make comments about its size. It was always in a joking manner with the assumption that of course she wouldn't mind because after all, they were just joking. Then one year at a family reunion, she said to the room at large, "You know, I almost didn't come this year because of all the comments about my nose. It seems my nose is the only thing you pay attention to." Everyone got uncomfortable and quiet.

Moving family or friendly relationships from being hurtfully teasing or sarcastic to being kind and loving can be an awkward and uncomfortable process. However, making fun of people is unkind. We are to refrain from *crude joking* (Ephesians 5:4).

The second thing to keep in mind is that a defensive reaction to being told our words were hurtful is basically saying, "I should be able to say whatever I want." That's just not true. God says no; words do have power. Jesus said, *I tell you, on the day of judgment people will give account for every careless word they speak* (Matthew 12:36).

In my experience, people are most cruel when they're embarrassed. If someone says something jokingly and it's taken seriously, yes, it puts a damper on the fun mood. However, fun should never come at someone else's expense. We teach people how to treat us by what we do and don't put up with. Declining to speak the truth in love allows poor behaviors to continue indefinitely, perhaps for a lifetime, for the sake of sparing a moment or two of awkwardness and discomfort.

Real fun is too important a factor in healing the brain and strengthening relationships to allow it to be replaced by sarcasm or hurtful joking that is labeled as fun. (We'll talk about this more when we look at opiates in particular.)

Another form of hustling, namely controlling speech, arises because of shame.

We fear others might find out the truth about us because of the things we've hidden. We're afraid others will find out what dirty deeds we've done. We fear this because we try to present a respectable image. I want to be thought well of. Even if I'm a two-bit, con artist and a bad mother, I don't want anyone to think so.

Out of shame, I may try to spin my words and presentation so your view of me won't be too bad. Here, again, is what Mother Teresa was talking about. If you're humble, disgrace can't touch you. If you're at least honest and brave with yourself and with the Lord, then you know who you are.

That's why confession can be so freeing – there's no more need to pretend.

If you know you are both sinner and saint, if you know you're saved only by the grace of God and the remission of sins atoned for on the cross of Calvary by our Lord and Savior Jesus Christ, then freedom lies in not having to pretend you are someone you're not.

Freedom lies in not having to pretend you've got it all together all the time. I'm not saying you should give yourself liberal permission to be unreliable or untrustworthy, but if someone says, "Wow! You totally overreacted to that," you can say, "I guess I did, didn't I? Give me a minute to apologize." You can say this sincerely because when you aren't expending tons of energy to seem perfect, it doesn't take a piece out of you to admit you were wrong.

Mother Teresa knew this mask of perfection well. She said, "Do not protect yourself behind your own dignity."

We hide behind a false sense of dignity to maintain the false image we've tried to create, the image of being worthy of great respect. If you know you're worthy of being treated with respect, you'll be able to ask for it calmly and lovingly and powerfully – with humility. When you see yourself as a child of the one true God, you know it's bad for you and bad for the other person to allow their disrespect to continue unchecked. You can speak up – calmly, lovingly, and humbly. If you're yelling about being disrespected, it says more about your insecurities than it does about the other person.

So, be honest and brave. We need to be willing to be honest and brave and give up the false sense of dignity and respectability we've clung to. We need to trade it in for being a sinner saved by grace and grateful to be alive and secure in who we are.

Moving back to gracious speech. Why does this matter in addiction?

Our Heavenly Father designed us to be in relationship, first to him and then to others. If you don't speak well, who will want to be around you? I don't mean you have to be a polished speaker who uses perfect grammar and fifty-cent words. I mean if you're always angry, always critical, and always seeing the worst in every situation, you're not enjoyable to be around.

Saying "Yeah, I know I'm a stick in the mud" is not acceptable. Change. Now. Do it. Stop being miserable. Stop being anxious.

When I say "stop being anxious," I'm not kidding, although it makes me smile to think of some reactions to the idea. *And which of you by being anxious can add a single hour to his span of life? If then you are not able to do as small a thing as that, why are you anxious about the rest?* (Luke 12:25-26). I've met many people who believe their anxiety is simply being "realistic." Yes, the sky could fall, but the Lord tells us we should *not be anxious about anything* (Philippians 4:6). *Do not be anxious about tomorrow* (Matthew 6:34). Jesus said, *Let not your hearts be troubled. Believe in God; believe also in me* (John 14:1).

Anxiety comes out in criticism and worrying, and it's not humble, nor does it give grace to those who hear.

When I say it isn't humble, I mean a lot of anxiety relates to pride and a loss of control, not life and death. If I'm anxious about losing my house, it's because I don't want to have to humble myself to live in an apartment or, heaven forbid, live with someone else and have to abide by their rules. And I'm worried about what it will say about me that I lost my home or my job. When my 12-year-old car starts making new sounds, being anxious will not change the mechanic's diagnosis. Prayer, however, will help me stay calm and make alternate plans, trusting that my heavenly Father knows what I need, and that there is nothing that will happen that he has not allowed. Trusting God means trusting him with everything – living situations, work, transportation, and even fun things like vacations.

> Anxiety comes out in criticism and worrying.

If you're what God calls "anxious" about a life-and-death situation (and some addictions are indeed life-and-death matters), then you're experiencing genuine fear. If that's the case, I urge you to read the Psalms, where David cried out to the Lord loudly and often because people were trying to kill him. If yours isn't a life-and-death situation, however, I urge you to consider the issues of pride or loss of control that may be working on you.

Why?

Because anxiety elevates stress. We already talked about how increased stress equals increased desire to engage in addictive behavior or substances. Stress produces cortisol, which does damage to your body over the long term. Stress greatly interferes with learning and memory.

Think about whether your anxiety relates to your self-image or self-esteem and how that fits in with being humble. Ask God to let you know if your God-given desire to do a good job ever becomes a prideful obsession to excel. Pray about whether your desire to be a leader has morphed into pride in your status as a leader.

A lot of anxiety is based on thinking if something happens or doesn't happen, it will be terrible. What's *terrible*? Does terrible mean you'll feel foolish? Does terrible mean you'll have to rely on someone else? Does terrible mean you'll no longer appear to have it all together? These are issues of pride. Does terrible mean you won't get what you want? Things won't go as planned? These are issues of control. God is in control, always. God's ways are not our ways.

WARNING! DANGER!

We're still talking about speech and dealing with others. Not acting in a prideful manner doesn't mean putting all your business on Front Street so everyone knows how you've messed up. It doesn't mean discussing all the troubles and trials of your life in loud and frequent conversation with anyone who'll listen. It doesn't mean treating other people as though they're the audience in a TV show where the baby mama's cousin's daughter was once the baby's dad.

Your speech should give grace, not nightmares, to those who hear it.

You need to reform your speech because addiction is a disease of isolation. *Whoever isolates himself seeks his own desire; he breaks out against all sound judgment* (Proverbs 18:1). Most addictions take place away from loved ones, away from the church, away from anyone of sound judgment who would urge you to stop. We are meant for relationships, and our speech impacts the quality of our relationships.

When I say addiction is a disease of isolation, I also mean that addiction keeps people from being present in their relationships. "Functional addicts" go to work, so if you're a functional addict, you might think, "I have a job. I'm not isolated."

Don't be fooled. Again, your addicted brain knows you need an income. This is not a happy coincidence. The fact that you're not homeless and not drinking malt liquor from a bottle in a brown paper bag doesn't mean your addiction "isn't that bad."

If you've read stuff written by older adults or can have honest conversations with them, you'll know how much they regret not focusing more on their relationships when there was still time.

I had a conversation with a hospice nurse who talked about the restless horror of people with unfinished business. People who have broken relationships may be lying on their death beds, filled with enough morphine to stop a tank, yet unable to find peace until that son, daughter, brother, sister, or friend comes to the bedside. Don't underestimate the damage a broken relationship can do. Seek to repair what you can, while you can.

It's hard to maintain a relationship, however, when you forget plans that were made. When, because you've had a bad day, you let yourself flake out and not show up for something you promised to attend. When the idea of going to your nephew's fifth grade band concert sounds about as much fun as getting a root canal, and maybe you show up, but you're very grumpy. Then you're even more annoyed when the person you showed up for doesn't appreciate your grumpy presence. None of these things makes for good relationships.

If I pour my heart out to you, and the next day you don't remember a thing I said because you went home and got high and forgot all about it, we haven't grown closer.

What will bridge the gap if you've hurt others in your addiction is going to be humility and gracious speech.

There's no immediate fix. No one owes you forgiveness or trust. Those must be earned and can be earned. It will take time, but it can be done.

You *can* heal your brain, get your raging thoughts of using under control, enjoy life, and look forward to long-lasting relationships with others. You *can* stop hustling and begin to use gracious and humble speech that will show others you're a comfortable joy to be around.

Just a few more things will have you on a solid path to repairing what has been broken in addiction. You *can* look forward to living the life you were created to live.

Chapter 11

Forgiving One Another

I'm convinced that many of us carry a great deal of sorrow around every day because we desire to hide behind our dignity.

Some addictions begin as a simple means of trying to experience pleasure. A little smoke, toot, shot, web surfing, harmless bet, little thrill, and it's all good. The use is based on a casual thought of what sounds good in the moment rather than an obsessive thought of "I need to use!"

There comes a point, though, where addiction sets in. With some, it's almost immediate. Whatever it was that you indulged in, it felt so good. In a life of zero self-discipline, the response was "Oh yeah, more, more, more!" With others, the shift from wanting to indulge to feeling a pressured need to indulge takes longer. The *Big Book* of Alcoholics Anonymous calls alcohol "cunning, baffling, powerful!" This is a good description for the way in which people can be surprised by the depth and extent of their addiction. Sometimes it just sneaks up on someone who is unaware of how their brain and thoughts are changing.

Years ago, I had a surgical procedure and was sent home with a painkiller. As with a lot of drugs, the painkiller didn't affect me the way it affects most people. Yes, it took away my sensation of pain. It also made me feel wonderfully in control, competent, and not the least bit anxious. (I tend to be anxious. I had panic attacks in my younger years. Miserable, awful, experiences I never want to have again.) These painkillers allowed me to feel like the absolute CEO of my little kingdom. The queen of the castle. I knew what to do and how to do it, and I had no doubts about it.

After a few days, though, I realized, "This is not me. This is not good." This particular brand of euphoria felt custom made for me and me alone, and I knew that was a red flag. I gave the pills up. I gave them to someone trustworthy and asked that person to make the pills disappear. I didn't trust myself not to root around in the trash and pull them back out again. I switched to an over-the-counter pain medication. I had to take things a little more slowly, but that was okay. At least I was me again. Even now, though, the mention of this pain medication stirs up a little longing in me because feeling that powerful and competent felt good. It was entirely fake, of course, and could have resulted in me neglecting my newborn child, but for a moment, it felt wonderful.

The person who has not practiced self-disciple, or who wishes not to, will defend themselves by saying, "My doctor prescribed these." Oh. Okay. Have you told your doctor they make you feel high? And did your doctor still approve of you using them?

Maybe there are other medications that would help you. Alcohol is a depressant, and people who stop drinking often find their anxiety level goes through the roof. Take the depressant away and anxieties and inhibitions sky-rocket. If you're so anxious you can't function, then a trial of an anti-anxiety medication may be in order.

However, this doesn't mean life-long dependence on anti-anxiety meds is the solution. It means you have a window of time in which to learn new skills for dealing with anxiety. Yes, some people are more anxious than others. At the other end of the spectrum, yes, some people have amazing coping skills. Most people are somewhere in between. If you started drinking at age fifteen to cope with life and you're now forty-five, then you still have the coping skills of a fifteen-year-old. You must do the work necessary to learn new coping skills appropriate for a forty-five-year-old.

You can't just pop pills and expect this will lead to the change you desire. The primary skills for dealing with anxiety are the same skills needed for overcoming addiction. It's important to find beauty, enjoy a meal, exercise, and practice stress management. The single most important thing to do, though, is to pray and take every thought captive, relying on God's promise to supply all our needs according to the riches in Christ Jesus for those who confess him as Lord and Savior (Philippians 4:19).

> You can't just pop pills and expect this will lead to the change you desire.

The physician who writes the prescription for anti-anxiety meds also has an interest in a couple of different things beyond your well-being. First, physicians are now judged by their patient reviews, which are used by insurance companies and hospitals to make decisions about the physicians' contracts. As I'm sure you can imagine, patients who expect drugs and don't get them give physicians bad reviews. This affects the physicians' livelihood and generates motivation to keep patients happy. It's a sad situation when *happy patients* means "over-medicated patients."

Beyond the reviews themselves, your physician is a human being who would prefer to avoid unpleasant scenes. Again, I'm sure you can imagine that patients expecting to receive drugs may protest loudly and cause a scene if they don't get their script. It may be easier to write a prescription than try to approach someone about lifestyle changes.

This is not to disparage physicians. Not at all. Physicians are people, too. Most want to move patients toward health in the best possible way. Yet the desire to *do justice* may lose out to the temptation to take the easy road, because that's human nature (Micah 6:8). *Enter by the narrow gate. For the gate is wide and the way is easy that leads to destruction, and those who enter by it are many* (Matthew 7:13).

If you're justifying long-term medication use on the grounds that your meds are prescribed by a doctor, your addicted brain is still loving the quick and easy solution. Who doesn't? Sure. But chances are you'll develop a tolerance for your anti-anxiety meds and take more than prescribed. Or, if you have a good relationship with your doctor, you may complain the meds aren't working as they once did, and your doctor may prescribe more medications or larger doses. In the meantime, chances are you won't be seeking to learn ways to cope without meds.

This isn't medical advice; it's addict behavior 101. If anti-anxiety, anti-depressant, anti-seizure, bi-polar, or pain meds are necessary for the short term, long term, or lifetime, pray and ask the Lord for wisdom and clarity regarding your medication. Even before your office visit with the prescriber, ask the Lord to direct your medical professional to only prescribe if needed, as needed.

If the medication is deeply meaningful and you never, ever want to be without it, though, that's a pretty strong emotional reaction to what should be one of many tools for recovery. You'll need to explore this with honesty and bravery. You can't just leave it all up to your doctor. *You* need to be the one to ask about lifestyle changes that can be more effective than any medication and move you towards greater health and healing overall.

I know we're supposed to be talking about forgiveness and dignity.

Here goes:

When was the last time you cried so hard in front of some-one that you shook and wailed and made weird noises? Your nose ran and your eyelids swelled up?

Pause here a minute and think about it. When was the last time you sobbed until you couldn't breathe? Was there anyone there to witness it? We can sometimes feel emotional pain as if the hurt happened yesterday, but if you can't show it, then here's where hiding behind your dignity harms you.

If you can't let go and sobbing is impossible, is it because you have no one you trust enough to be this vulnerable in front of? Is it because you're so distanced from yourself you've closed it off?

In the Old Testament, people grieved by wearing sackcloth and daubing themselves with ashes, wailing and weeping, and sometimes tearing their hair. God understands. He knows when we cry (Psalm 56:8). Jesus himself wept (John 11:35). David and Jonathan, the best friends in the Bible, wept together when they realized Jonathan's father wanted David dead (1 Samuel 20:32-41). Job wept so much his face became flushed (Job 16:16). Peter wept bitterly when he realized Jesus's prediction of betrayal was true (Matthew 26:75). As Paul was about to head off to more places where he would be imprisoned, he spoke to the elders of the church of Ephesus of how they had witnessed his tears and trials (Acts 20:19-23).

No one escapes grief in this life, but I can't tell you how many times I've had people apologize to me for their tears. My goal was to create a space that felt safe enough for tears, and still they apologized. We're so distanced from grief it can be awkward to see someone overcome by it. For the person griev-ing to be embarrassed by the way they've showed their grief is another sadness.

We want so badly to cling to our false sense of dignity.

Beyond our personal concept of dignity, which can be just a mask of misplaced pride, the general concept of dignity is being twisted in our political climate. The illusion of dignity encourages voters in some states to approve actions that don't respect what God's Word says about who we are. We're leaving behind a concept of dignity that says life itself is valuable and instead embracing the idea that only a certain attainable lifestyle is valuable. I'm talking now about the way in which we depart this life.

Oregon was the first state to allow physician-assisted suicide. Most people think that means a physician may help someone who is in great pain to die. However, most of the people who asked for the suicide cocktail were not in great pain.[12] They were only afraid they would be. They wanted to avoid any chance of dying without "dignity." They were tired of living without a better quality of life, and they weren't willing to wait until the Lord took them home. This is a separate issue from not being artificially kept alive by machines. Physician-assisted suicide agrees with intentionally ending life.

Many people have read that suicides within the military have increased in recent years. Most people who are aware of this fact assume it's a result of being deployed in Iraq or Afghanistan. We think veteran suicide is a result of the horror of war taking a toll on the veteran's psyche, but this is not, in fact, the chief cause. Between 2001 and 2007, almost 77 percent of suicides were by personnel who had never been deployed.[13]

As a country, we've embraced a muddled and sad sense of dignity. We rationalize the idea it's better to die with dignity than to bravely face life as it comes. Since Oregon passed its assisted-suicide law, five more states have followed in kind. As a country, more and more people agree we should give depressed

---

12   Lynne Terry, "Study: Oregon patients using physician-assisted suicide steadily increase," *The Oregonian/OregonLive* (April 6, 2017), accessed August 15, 2017, https://tinyurl.com/ybs5elwg.

13   Patricia Kime, "Study: No link between combat deployment and suicides," *MilitaryTimes.com* (April 1, 2015), https://tinyurl.com/y717moxm.

and frightened people a suicide cocktail when the end is near to avoid all the unpleasantness of their inevitable death. Similarly, looking at the rate of abortion, you realize that as a country, we say those who are inconvenienced by any unborn life should have the right to end it on demand.

When we look at "dignity" in this manner and consider our increasingly non-judgmental attitude towards ending life, it's no wonder people hide addictions because of shame. Many people find themselves so ashamed of their addiction they think they would rather die than take positive, public steps to fight it. Many are so afraid of pain they think they would rather die than endure it. And many, many people can't even talk about the depth of their fear of the hold the addiction has on them, because to do so would mean uncontrollable sobbing, moaning sounds of a grief that has no words, runny noses, overflowing saliva, and a feeling that they're breaking apart. All the while, your brain is telling you, "This is so undignified, you've got to stop. Stop this now! Get a hold of yourself!" A voice inside your head whispers, "Maybe it would be better if I died."

No! Don't die, grieve! Cry. Sob. Grieve for the things you've done and the things that have been done to you. Grieve the losses you've experienced. Grieve the loss of your own innocence and the loss of loved ones. Tear your clothes, beat your fists on the ground, yell at God, "Why? Why?" Tell him how much it hurts. *The Lord is near to the brokenhearted and saves the crushed in spirit* (Psalm 34:18). Tell him you can't breathe for the pain; tell him how much you hate it. He won't repair what you won't even admit is broken. *The sacrifices of God are a broken spirit; a broken and contrite heart, O God, you will not despise* (Psalm 51:17). *Blessed are those who mourn, for they shall be comforted* (Matthew 5:4). God can't comfort you if you won't grieve.

Hang on to what makes you a human being, formed in the image of God. Don't set it aside in some badly misplaced sense of pride and dignity. In spite of all its pain, embrace life for the joy and true dignity of living the way we were created to live.

And if someone witnesses your grieving and is a little weirded out by it, don't apologize. If it happened in the middle of the workday, you might wish the timing had been better, but don't apologize. We are to be tender-hearted (Ephesians 4:32). We are to be comforters (2 Corinthians 1:3-4). It's good for us to be tender-hearted comforters. It's bad to be so uncomfortable with grief that we avoid it and the person who feels it. This avoidance sends the message that a person's grief makes them unlovable – a message that only intensifies the hurt they feel.

Dignity involves being worthy of respect. We're worthy of respect because we're made in God's image. No amount of shuddering, spirit-crushing sobs and no weight of pain or anguish changes the fact that you are a child of God and worthy of respect. Your dignity is not diminished by your tears. Your dignity will never be a reflection of your physical body with all its failings. Rather, it's a mirror of the status of your soul and your relationship with God and others as one created in his image.

We are sinners and saints. We are children of God and slaves to sin. We seek to do good and often accomplish little. This is who we are. In the midst of this, we can have unimagined joy and gratitude and relationships so full of love it feels the heart may burst – as long as there is forgiveness. After grieving and giving up false dignity, seek to forgive and seek forgiveness from others.

A couple of myths about forgiveness:

It's a once-and-done kind of thing.
No. Forgiveness can be a process. You can think you've forgiven someone and later find yourself very angry because a new event has reminded you of what that person did.

Forgiveness means reconciliation.
No. Forgiving someone doesn't mean staying close to them if they're abusive and aren't taking any action to change their ways. This is a case-by-case situation, but if you're in an abusive relationship, particularly if it's physically abusive, this is not what you deserve. Deciding to forgive doesn't mean that you've agreed to put up with that behavior. Jesus says if someone sins against you, rebuke them, and if they repent, forgive them (Luke 17:3). To repent is to turn away. Simply saying "I'm sorry" is meaningless if the speaker isn't trying to change. And forgiving someone without telling them that in some way they've sinned against you doesn't solve the problem.

Forgiveness does mean giving up any thoughts of vengeance.
I used to think vengeance meant revenge on a grand scale. *Vengeance is mine, I will repay, says the Lord* (Romans 12:19). The word *vengeance* made me think of chariots of fire and earthquakes and famine and plagues. Being a peace-loving person, I was happy to leave all that to God. Or so I thought. I was unhappy when I realized I actually do like a little bit of vengeance on the side.

What do I mean? I mean that if you apologize, and I graciously accept your apology, then I have a tendency to think you should still act sorry for at least a little while after. See, I have in my mind an idea of how you'd behave if you were truly sorry. If you don't do what I think you ought to do, I'm very suspicious of your claim to regret whatever it was you did to me.

This is vengeance – punishment for a perceived injury. This

idea I have of how you ought to look a little sad, be nice to me, or hold off on returning to normal for a time is not forgiveness. This is wanting my pound of flesh before I agree to treat you lovingly again. If I have this idea in my mind, I haven't forgiven you.

If I've received a sincere apology from someone who's trying to do better, that needs to be enough. We should return to normal right then. I don't deserve extra special treatment for a set time because I was hurt. I don't have the right to demand you give me extra special treatment because you hurt me. That would be seeking vengeance.

I've met a lot of people who've said, "I can never forgive ____ [fill in the blank]."

That's a problem. Any way you might finish that sentence is a problem, because *as the Lord has forgiven you, so you also must forgive* (Colossians 3:13). If you forgive others, your heavenly Father will forgive you, but if you don't forgive, you won't be forgiven (Matthew 6:14-15). We are to pray that the Lord will forgive us as we forgive others (Matthew 6:12). The measure we use will be the measure used for us (Matthew 7:2).

Are you sure you even noticed every time you hurt someone?

People say, "But for the grace of God, that would be me," with the idea in mind that God has kept them from a fate worse than death. Yet when we look at others and struggle to forgive, there's this idea that we would never have done what they did.

Okay. Well. There are things you've done that others would not have. Are you sure you know how much damage you've done to others? You're not them. Have you always been brave enough to ask, "How badly did I hurt you?" Are you sure you even noticed every time you hurt someone?

We like to imagine we have a mind like a steel trap when it comes to certain events. We like to believe we know exactly who said what and when and how and in what tone and what our response was. That's just not true. If you've ever had a conversation with someone about an event that happened in the past, you know that's not true. There are details that get lost in the re-telling or that are reported differently even minutes after the event occurred. Our brains literally cannot store a second-by-second record of our lives.

For myself, I would never want to walk into a room full of people that I've hurt and know that we were there to discuss all the ways in which I hurt them. I'm grateful for all the sins I haven't committed (mostly because I haven't been sufficiently tempted, I'm afraid), and sadly, I'm grateful to not know of all those I've hurt with careless words and thoughtless actions I don't even remember.

In Luke 18, Jesus tells the parable of the Pharisee and the tax collector. Pharisees were the church leaders. Tax collectors were government-sponsored con men. The Pharisee prayed, *"God, I thank you that I am not like other men, extortioners, unjust, adulterers, or even like this tax collector."* The tax collector prayed, *"God, be merciful to me, a sinner!"* (Luke 18:11, 13). Jesus said that of the two men, it was the tax collector who went home right with God.

We look at others' lives and arrogantly assume we would have made difference choices. We think we would've chosen differently even though we have no knowledge of what choices this person even faced or what consequences they imagined for the different choices they had. I must give account for *my* life. I try and pray to have only compassion for those who must give account for things I have so fortunately not had the temptation or opportunity to do.

I never want to experience the kind of life someone must have lived to see shooting up heroin as an option. I never want to be such a thrill-seeker that I lose thousands of dollars on a bet. I hope I never again get so anxious I think I need a drink because otherwise I can't relax. Are these actions sinful? Yes, of course they are. So is spreading gossip. Gossip is included in a list of sins that includes hatred of God, murder, and faithlessness (Romans 1:29-31). James, the brother of Jesus, said that if a person who considers themselves religious doesn't keep a tight rein on their tongue, their religion is worthless (James 1:26). We all sin, and we can only be thankful there are sins we haven't committed.

If you were abused as a child, you may have a lot of resentment and difficulty with personal relationships. Loving someone means wanting our heavenly Father's best for that person. It means acting and behaving in a way that shows your good will. We can agree the person who abused you didn't truly love you. But if you're ever to stop living under the shadow of past hurt and betrayal, you have to forgive the person who was too broken and too full of sin to love as they should have done.

Forgiving means forgiving the coward who didn't help you when they knew you needed help. It means forgiving the person who carelessly shamed you. It means forgiving the person who was too weak to resist temptation. It means setting aside the arrogant thought that you would have done things differently.

Forgiving means letting go of your desire for vengeance, your longing to see the other person punished, or your hope to inflict punishment on them. It means letting go of your victim status and saying, "How sad it is this happened to me, and how sad this person was so unkind."

Why? So you can love. So you can love generously without the deep-seated resentment and mistrust that lingers when you don't forgive. It doesn't matter if the person you can't forgive has long passed away. You'll have trouble trusting anyone who reminds you of someone you haven't forgiven. You can't carry resentment inside and be open to the vulnerabilities of love.

Erica Jong says, "Love is everything it's cracked up to be. It's worth fighting for, being brave for. That's why people are so cynical about it. It's easier to stand back being a cynic than to risk taking that leap."[14] In the seventeenth century John Dryden stated, "Love is love's reward."

Whether it's the love of friends or spouses or children, love is *it*. Love is everything. *A new commandment I give to you, that you love one another: just as I have loved you, you also are to love one another* (John 13:34).

You can't be loving, tender-hearted, and forgiving if you're hanging on to past hurts.

> You can't be loving, tender-hearted, and forgiving if you're hanging on to past hurts.

Now there's a lot of talk today about forgiving yourself, especially in recovery. This is not biblical. *If we confess our sins, he* [God] *is faithful and just to forgive our sins and to cleanse us from all unrighteousness* (1 John 1:9). It's God who does this. Not us.

God forgives us, and we are forgiven. You ought also to ask forgiveness from people you've hurt – being honest and brave and not making excuses or justifying. Just say, "I did this, and I know it hurt you, and I apologize and hope you'll forgive me."

From here, then, know that lingering guilt and shame are tools of the Enemy, to keep you from being able to enjoy the life God has planned for you. They are also emotions that keep us from the kingdom work God has for us. Lingering guilt and shame keep us from speaking up about injustice or witnessing to others. When you're loaded with guilt and shame, you hesitate to speak the truth in love. You hesitate to share the good news of the gospel of Jesus Christ and the work of the Holy Spirit in restoring your soul, because someone might look at you and

---

14   This quote is attributed to Erica Jong. It is a rephrasing of a statement made in *Inventing Memory: A Novel of Mothers and Daughters*. The quote can be found by an unsourced contributor at https://en.wikiquote.org/wiki/Talk:Erica_Jong.

say, "Yeah, right." If you're carrying a load of guilt and shame, you'll feel silly and embarrassed for having said a word.

Jesus said that *everyone who practices sin is a slave to sin* (John 8:34). But, *if you abide in my word . . . you will know the truth, and the truth will set you free* (John 8:31-32).

The truth is there is no one who is righteous. Jesus came for sinners (Luke 5:32). Confessing your sin is agreeing you're a sinner, and keeping this in mind makes it a whole lot easier to be humble. On the other hand, persistently wallowing in guilt and shame is very counter-productive to the idea of being free. The answer is not to forgive yourself. The answer is to realize that if God has forgiven you, you're forgiven. Period. The end. Continued guilt will only keep you from things like disciplining your children when they need it, because you feel bad about the times when you did something wrong. But your children will pay the price for your reluctance. It will keep you from telling your spouse that their words hurt your feelings, because you feel bad about all the times you hurt them. But your marriage will pay the price for your lack of honesty. Continued guilt keeps you from speaking the truth in love. By making you feel unworthy, it keeps you from undertaking the task of doing the work the Lord has prepared for you.

If the Lord has forgiven you and set a task before you, he's decided you're ready; you are the chosen one for this task, and who are you to say differently? (Ephesians 2:10). You can't allow the Enemy, your own shame, or others, especially unbelieving others, to allow you to think you're too damaged to serve the kingdom of God.

I write the above in tears because as much as I know the truth of what I've written, I also know how hard it is. I have an advanced education. I know lots of things, but when it comes right down to it, I'm afraid. I'm afraid people will read this and think, "What nonsense." I'm afraid people who have spent their lives dealing with addictions will say this is useless advice. I'm afraid my colleagues who work with people who have addictions will say I'm wrong, wrong, wrong.

Yet despite my fear, despite feeling silly and thinking, "Who am I to imagine the Lord has a message for me to share?" I'm doing it. With a sense of urgency, I'm sharing the truth I've been blessed to receive. My heavenly Father who loves me would have me share the joy of that love. Jesus loves me. This I know for sure now.

But speaking of not knowing and possibly being wrong, my favorite written prayer is this one by Thomas Merton. He was well acquainted with how we don't live just by clear rules, we live in constant relationship with our heavenly Father. He knew what it was like to not know and yet to trust.

> *My Lord God, I have no idea where I am going. I do not see the road ahead of me. I cannot know for certain where it will end. Nor do I really know myself, and the fact that I think that I am following your will does not mean that I am actually doing so. But I believe that the desire to please you does in fact please you. And I hope I have that desire in all that I am doing. I hope that I will never do anything apart from that desire. And I know that if I do this, you will lead me by the right road, though I may know nothing about it. Therefore will I trust you always, though I may seem to be lost and in the shadow of death. I will not fear, for you are ever with me, and you will never leave me to face my perils alone.*[15]

---

15 Thomas Merton, "The Love of Solitude," *Thoughts in Solitude,* Part 2 chapter 2 (Boston: Shambhala Publications, by arrangement with Farrar, Straus and Giroux, 1956), 89.

Chapter 12

Our Opiate Epidemic

When a person develops an addiction, it alters the chemical structure of the brain. In other words, the brain changes.

The Lord designed our brains to be amazing and complex organs that sustain life and produce words for speech and prayer as well as reflexes to protect us. We are *fearfully and wonderfully made* (Psalm 139:14).

This book is a not a scholarly work on how addiction changes the brain. There are thoughts and theories and facts galore that you can read at your leisure if you want to get a better understanding of exactly how and why the brain changes. There is one work, however, I want to discuss here.

Jaak Panksepp (a man who has now passed away but who studied emotions for forty years) and Lucy Biven (former head of the Department of Child and Adolescent Psychotherapy at the Leicestershire National Health Service in England) co-authored a book titled *The Archaeology of Mind: Neuroevolutionary Origins of Human Emotions*. Truth is from God, no matter the source. Panksepp and Biven's evolutionary perspective does not alter the facts of their research, only the interpretation of those facts. Viewed from a biblical perspective, their findings underscore the importance of living life according to God's plan for us.

Panksepp and Biven discuss how people who become addicted to opiates lose their ability to play and have fun. The brain changes so profoundly that the capacity for spontaneous joy is washed away in the opioid flood. Play only occurs in the presence of a low amount of opiates. How low? The amount that comes from a healthy brain responding to the presence of others.[16] Our brains produce low amounts of opiates from welcome touch, such as a hug or a *holy kiss* (1 Thessalonians 5:26; Romans 16:16; Luke 7:45). When we feel safe and secure, we can play. We can laugh, have fun, and enjoy the company of others.

Play needs to be incorporated a great deal more into recovery. We need the joy and the laughter of it. We also need the practice of losing graciously and not letting our egos rule. Competitive play can bring out an ugly side in people. A pastor I know told a story of being called aside lovingly by a brother in Christ for his aggressiveness. He wanted to win so much he made some in the youth group cry. Oops!

Play can feel very foolish to the loser if you focus on losing. These are things to work through, though, with a goal of sharing connection with others. The things that can complicate play shouldn't be obstacles to it. In fact, they should be learning opportunities. Don't focus on losing. Call out the super aggressive player. Proceed in the knowledge that play is important.

I can't emphasize enough – PLAY! Buy some bubble liquid. Get a board game that depends on luck and not skill. Set aside the misplaced dignity that keeps you from being able to play and have fun. Get over the idea that you'll lose – because you

---

16   Jaak Panksepp and Lucy Biven, *The Archaeology of Mind: Neuroevolutionary Origins of Human Emotions* (W. W. Norton & Company, 2012), 350-355.

will! Learn to enjoy playing anyway. There's no fun in being standoffish, cynical, jaded, and bitter. Refusing to join in the fun highlights a person's isolation and loneliness.

Get off your phone! Remember how we talked earlier about being created to desire and appreciate the undivided attention of another? Remember me talking about that time I was telling a story and my listener quit listening? Don't think being on your phone is no big deal. Outside of a genuine emergency, the phone serves as a tool for instant gratification. Also, if you and I are together, but you're on your phone,

Get off your phone!

it's only natural for me to assume you've got something going on that's more important than I am. You, on the other hand, may be assuming I understand there are a couple of things you need to get out of the way. Either way, the situation is ripe for misunderstanding and hurt feelings. Being on your phone in the presence of others is a barrier to good relationship.

We're created with a need to be relational, to feel that we matter to others, and to experience being loved. There's no love flowing from the smartphone or the person using it in the company of others. Learn to wait. Whatever the phone call is about, if it's not an emergency, it can wait.

Having five hundred social media friends without one live person to spend time with is sad and painful, and it's lonelier than most people will admit. If you don't put down your phone and communicate in person, face to face, you won't be able to fully experience love as God designed you to. Put down your phone and commit to play!

Do charades. Quit taking yourself so seriously and be intentionally playful. Be brave. Tell your family that board games are important for your recovery.

If you're early in recovery, I know you won't feel like it. You might consider the idea and groan out loud. Do it anyway.

What fun is life without fun? And like confidence, you need to fake it until you make it. By that I mean the best way to feel confident is to pretend you feel confident; hold your head up, make eye contact, and act the way a capable person acts. Do the same with having fun. Paste a smile on your face, laugh when others laugh, think pleasant thoughts, and resist all self-talk along the lines of "Oh, I hate this, this is so dumb; there are a million places I'd rather be."

Use your body to convey the thoughts you want to have in your brain. When you feel anxious, lift your head up, pull your shoulders back, and breathe deeply. When **Use your body to** you want to appear confident, adopt the **influence your brain** same posture, stand tall, and smile. When **for the better.** you're ready to play, it's time to smile, look around, laugh, and bounce on your feet. Use your body to influence your brain for the better. Your brain chemicals will shift gears and catch on. Do this.

Why? Because engaging your brain to heal and produce God-given, feel-good chemicals is necessary for recovery. It's true that healing can take place without your dedicated effort, because God designed our bodies to be self-regulating. However, if you don't make an effort towards healing, the process will take longer.

Also, if you don't do what you can to heal your brain, I say you must be finding some reward in staying a victim and a slave to sin. If you're unwilling to take steps that, according to the truth of the Word of God, are critical to our very being, perhaps you're afraid of who you would be if you changed. It's understandable to wonder, "Who will I be if I'm not the person I've been?" But trust God; he knows the answer. Be brave.

Jesus came so that we may have life and have it abundantly, to the full, with joys we've never even imagined (John 10:10; Ephesians 3:19-21). But you can't have this wonderful experience by clinging to your old life and your old ways. In Christ, we become a new creation, and the old is put away (2 Corinthians 5:17).

Jesus got a reputation for being a glutton and a drunkard because of the time he spent eating and drinking with others (Matthew 11:19). No, Jesus was not a drunk, and the Bible certainly doesn't advise us to get drunk – quite the opposite, in fact. *Wine is a mocker, strong drink a brawler, and whoever is led astray by it is not wise* (Proverbs 20:1). *And do not get drunk with wine, for that is debauchery, but be filled with the Spirit* (Ephesians 5:18). But a good meal in the company of treasured others can be fun; it can even be play.

Storytelling is great play. Storytelling is how we relate best to others. We may not remember the exact words later, but we remember the emotion. If it's a good story, even if it's not our story, it's fun to repeat. Jesus spoke in stories called parables. Two thousand years later, we know that stories are the most easily remembered form of communication. In the Old Testament, God reminds the Israelites over and over again to tell their children the story of his grace and goodness in getting them out of Egypt. Tell stories, but take turns, and be generous in the time you give to others.

If being around alcohol is difficult for you, don't spend time around people who continue to drink. They are not your friends, and they love their right to be intoxicated more than they love you. Yes, that sounds harsh, but if you knew someone had a deathly allergy to cheese, wouldn't you go without it when they were around? We all ought to be entirely capable of having great fun without the use of mood-altering chemicals.

Make it a point to greet people as they come in the door. Acknowledge them as if they matter. Every time. Don't start up with holy kisses, especially if you never have before or if the other person is a member of the opposite sex, but at least try a fist-bump like you mean it.[17]

Smile. Smile often. There's abundant research on a smile known as the "Duchenne smile." (Duchenne was a bit of a mad scientist, but his research was good.) This smile is the one that reaches your eyes. This smile, he said, reflects the "sweet emotions of the soul."[18] When your smile reaches your eyes, you send the message to your brain and body that there's sweetness and goodness in life. In fact, you can't smile this sincerely without thinking good thoughts. This is the smile that communicates genuine care for another.

When you focus on another person, make eye contact, and convey genuine care, two things happen. One, you show the love of Christ to the other person. You see them. You really see them. Two, you communicate to yourself that you are a person who cares. This is vital because the spiritual battle of addiction makes it entirely too tempting to throw up your hands and say, "I don't care anymore."

If you begin to play, your brain will begin to produce the low-dose opiates that go along with feeling good. If you begin to play, you'll send the message to your anxiety-filled brain that no, today is not the day to worry about things you can't control. If you begin to play, you'll take yourself less seriously, you'll find it easier to be humble, and your body and brain will work together in rewarding ways. It will be easier to find beauty, enjoy meals, and take pleasure in the companionship of imperfect others whom God has put in your life. Sooner rather than later, feeling good will feel familiar and won't require such effort.

It's a sad fact of our broken lives that to fully enjoy

17   John Piper, "The Holy Kiss – Relevant Today or Not?" *Ask Pastor John* (December 3, 2015), accessed August 16, 2017, https://tinyurl.com/ycc37ewn.

18   Eric Jaffe, "The Psychological Study of Smiling," *Observer* 23, no. 10 (University of Minnesota, Association for Psychological Science, December 2010), https://tinyurl.com/yccck5bv.

God-honoring, God-given sources of pleasure takes work. To enjoy a meal without overeating. To enjoy work, family, and home life yet keep them in balance. To enjoy exercise without obsession. To enjoy talking to others without gossiping and backbiting. The more good behaviors are practiced and put in place, however, the more natural and freely enjoyable they become. You'd think making good, healthy decisions ought to be easier, but they're much harder to make than selfish, self-destructive ones. The payoff for the effort, though, is divine!

If you're alone and lonely and there's no one to have fun with, I suggest you buy some bubble liquid and make bubbles because, really, they reflect rainbows, which are God's promise to us, and rainbows are beautiful. God said, *I have set my bow in the cloud, and it shall be a sign of the covenant between me and the earth* (Genesis 9:13). Go to the park, or your backyard, or your front steps – just you and your bubbles – and enjoy feeling like a little kid for a while.

Chapter 13

Loving Someone with an Addiction

I f you're the person who loves someone with an addiction, you know how one minute there's a hope for the future that makes your heart soar, and the next minute there's head-shaking despair over the foolishness of your belief. One day there's so much frustration you may think you don't care if something terrible happens to that person. The next day, you've heard nothing from them, and you're terrified something bad has happened to them.

Two things:

First, if your loved one is in recovery, it's tempting to think that if they don't use or indulge in the addiction anymore, all will be well. If you've read the previous pages, however, you know this isn't true. If you haven't read any of the previous pages, then I'll summarize: The behaviors that go along with addiction are used in order to gain whatever is desired. That means that any lying, hiding, evasive, non-sharing behaviors are still going to be there and will show up when there's something that person desires. The something may be avoidance of pain or responsibility or criticism or argument. These behaviors will take time to unlearn. It will take time (how long a time depends on the severity of the addiction) for your loved one to learn how to be honest, open, and engaged. The person in recovery is learning a whole new way of life, not simply (yeah, like it's ever simple) a way to live without addiction.

Second, there will be times when your loved one's changes irritate you. You may be the most loving person in the world, but you can only be so grateful for someone's recovery for so long. Eventually, your loved one will say or do something that will irritate you to no end. It may even be because of their new recovery. If you walk on eggshells trying to keep the peace, protect the other person's happiness, do everything you can do to support their recovery, you set yourself up for resentment. There needs to be an agreement between you and your loved one that you will both do your best to be honest and brave and to speak truth in love with a goal of giving grace to each other.

> **The person in recovery is learning a whole new way of life.**

What does this look like? Maybe in the past you've teased your loved one about being disorganized, and one day your loved one says, "You know, that hurts my feelings, because I'm trying to be better organized."

"Ooohhh! That hurts your feelings, huh? Last week you made fun of me for being afraid of a spider. Normal people are afraid of spiders. Normal people don't lose their keys every doggone day!"

Uh-oh. A response like that shows you've been carrying a grudge and harboring resentment. While understandable, especially if you've spent night after night wondering if your loved one is even going to live, it means you're struggling with forgiveness. Resentment always leaps out sideways in the heat of the moment. The key is to recognize it for what it is, to be ready for it to happen, and most importantly, to be prepared to apologize sincerely when it does. This is grace.

Whatever someone has done in the past, if you're still sticking around, then you've made the choice to do so. It's up to you to work on forgiving and loving the addicted person as you both work on following Jesus into the life God has designed for you.

If you can't do your part, then what kind of punishment would you have the addicted person suffer? The answer is buried in your grief over lost time, lost dreams, lost happiness. Often, what we most want is an apology that acknowledges our pain. You may need to grieve what you've lost before you can forgive, but your resentments are your own to work through. If you take them out on your loved one who is working on recovery, you undermine their recovery, your joy, and the future of your relationship.

Chapter 14

A Brief Word about Sexuality

First Corinthians chapter 7 lays it out. It's better to marry than to burn, and each spouse should willingly give conjugal rights to the other. Sex should never be used as a weapon or withheld because of petty anger or perceived slights. The expression of love in sexuality is reserved for marriage. To put it plainly, if you're married, your sexual pleasure should always involve your spouse – live and in person. Sexual love should not be withheld except by mutual consent for a time in which you both wish to engage in prayer and fasting. The purpose of deliberately abstaining from sexual pleasure with your spouse should only be to focus on the Lord.

If sex isn't your thing, you shouldn't feel pressured to get married.

Sexuality outside of marriage is sin, and it's going to cause problems. You may think you can handle the problems it causes, but I urge you with all heartfelt compassion to consider what God's best plan is for your life. If you're caught in sexual sin, cry out to the Lord to deliver you from it. There are many Christians working to help others stay free from sexual sin, offering solid advice for avoiding temptation, and even providing resources to guard your electronics from pornography. Don't hide behind your dignity if this is an issue you need help with.

The Song of Solomon shows God's heart for marriage and sexuality. God's design is for our mind and body to become one – with *one* other. Anything else hurts us in body, mind, and spirit.

There's nothing so romantic and inspiring as a married couple who are in love and who show this love in kind words, frequent touches, lingering eye contact. Scripture says this love, this romance, points us towards the picture of Jesus Christ and the church (Ephesians 5:32). That's the beauty of marriage as God has designed it to be.

The important thing is to honor God's best for us, whether it's in marriage or in a single life.

Chapter 15

Traditional Treatment
for Addiction

N othing I have written here is meant to suggest traditional treatment is unnecessary.

Some people come to Jesus, and they are delivered. Healed from addiction. Some believers suggest this is how it is for everyone who truly comes to Jesus. I think they forget parts of Scripture, such as where Paul is writing to the church in Corinth telling them they're still in the flesh and are only babes in Christ (1 Corinthians 3:1-3). Not everyone is instantly relieved of all addictive behaviors when they pray to be delivered, just as not everyone is instantly relieved of all physical problems when they pray to be healed. We don't see the whole picture as God does, so we can't know why our story is different from that of others.

The Alcoholics Anonymous *Big Book* suggests that a person may lose all desire to drink and yet struggle mightily with all the behaviors that went with drinking. The famous twelve-step plan of recovery includes taking a daily inventory and being always prepared to admit and apologize for wrongs committed on an ongoing basis because there *will* be wrongs committed on an ongoing basis.

Since instant transformation through prayer isn't every believer's story, treatment should always be an option.

WARNING! DANGER!

Formal treatment definitely needs to be part of the picture if you have a problem with alcohol, opiates or other narcotics, benzodiazepines or other anti-anxiety meds, or other health issues. This is because quitting cold turkey may cause complications like, um, death. You need medically supervised detox.

Without life-threatening issues, you may have reason to think beginning one-on-one counseling is a better place for you to start. I recommend working with a person you feel led to trust. I also recommend praying. A lot.

I would say start with a Christian counselor, except that I recently read some rather shocking statistics. According to the Pew Research Center, 70.6 percent of Americans still call themselves Christian in 2014, but only approximately 63 percent of these same people absolutely believe God exists.[19] The rest aren't so sure. Also, while a large number of people do consider themselves to be born-again or evangelical Christians, this includes a significant number of Mormons and Jehovah's Witnesses.

If you're seeking a counselor who's trained in the authority of Scripture, the Association of Certified Biblical Counselors (ACBC) may have someone in your area. There are other organizations that also believe the authority of Scripture is sufficient for counseling and have trained counselors.

Please understand that without a certifying organization,

---

19 Pew Research Center, "Religious Landscape Study," conducted June 4 to September 30, 2014, accessed August 16, 2017, https://tinyurl.com/ldnxabw.

the fact that someone calls themselves a Christian doesn't mean they counsel based on the authority of God's Word.

The Bible says we're Christians if we are disciples, followers of Jesus Christ (Acts 11:26). The Bible tells us Jesus was both God and man; he died, and he was resurrected. Being the sinless and only begotten Son of God, he paid the price for our sins (John 3:16). The apostle Paul tells us we *were bought with a price. So glorify God in your body* (1 Corinthians 6:20). The process of becoming more like Christ is called sanctification. And it is a process. We're not immediately just like Jesus once we accept him as Lord and Savior, although we are counted as righteous and justified in God's eyes. We also become heirs to the kingdom of God, as Jesus is (Titus 3:4-7).

> There is nothing that wanting ever made true.

The Bible is the Word of God, and it speaks not only of our creation but of our eternity (Genesis and Revelation). The world will say the Bible is contradictory and inconsistent and not trustworthy. But if you read the Bible and pray for understanding, the Holy Spirit will lead you to know it's the Word of God and is absolutely to be trusted.

There are people who say those who believe in God only believe because they want there to be a God. People say believers just like the idea of heaven. To them, I would say that this wanting doesn't matter at all. It doesn't change anything. Whether you want there to be a God or no God, heaven or hell, righteousness or sin, is not the point. There is nothing that wanting ever made true.

I've also known many whose pride interferes with their faith. My own pride interfered with my faith for a long time. Searching the internet, I find that most criticisms of the Bible are smug, prideful assertions of being too intelligent or too educated to believe in its truth. That's funny to me. Shepherds from two thousand years ago are laughed about, yet the pyramids are solemnly explained as having been constructed by aliens. We look for ways to not believe the Word of God, but the Lord calls us to him for every good thing. Being too proud to believe, we seek to escape the truth and become too stiff-necked to turn to the Lord for help.

You'd be foolish to let the world, your unbelieving friends or family, or your pride get in the way of allowing God's Word to do the work on your heart and soul and mind that it promises to do. *For the word of God is living and active, sharper than any two-edged sword, piercing to the division of soul and of spirit, of joints and of marrow, and discerning the thoughts and intentions of the heart* (Hebrews 4:12). *Likewise the Spirit helps us in our weakness. For we do not know what to pray for as we ought, but the Spirit himself intercedes for us with groanings too deep for words* (Romans 8:26).

The Bible is the Word of God. Any book other than the Bible is not God's Word. God's Word will work with the Holy Spirit to convict you of past sin, so that you can repent and ask forgiveness, be forgiven, and continue in sanctification and real freedom. God's Word will work with the Holy Spirit so you can confidently approach the throne of grace with the promises of God in your prayers (Hebrews 4:16; John 14:13). You'll experience more answered prayer as God's Word works with the Holy Spirit to ensure you ask rightly, in accordance with the will of God instead of wrongly to satisfy your own desires (James 4:3). The answered prayer will then increase your faith, and you'll be caught in the shining light of God's glory instead of being caught in sin. Others will see your light shine from a great distance and give glory to God for your good works (Matthew 5:16). This is how you know the Bible is the Word of God. You will experience the truth for yourself if you step out in faith, read the Bible for yourself, and pray for understanding.

Some people say all the different translations make the Bible untrustworthy. If you research, though, and spend time learning why Bible scholars say we can trust the Bible is God's Word, you'll know how greatly the world lies. Of course it does! The world is still under the rule of the Evil One who is the father of lies. *When he lies, he speaks out of his own character, for he is a liar and the father of lies* (John 8:44). And, *the god of this world has blinded the minds of the unbelievers, to keep them from seeing the light of the gospel of the glory of Christ* (2 Corinthians 4:4). But if you don't read the Bible in prayer for understanding, and you do listen to what the world says, then it will be all too easy for you to accept that those who calls themselves Christians probably are, even if their beliefs don't match the truth of God's Word.

We'd like to excuse beliefs that don't match the truth of God's Word with the idea that trying to be good must count for something. We'd like to think that a person who wants to do good at least has Christian values.

The thing is (and here's that bit of logic again), if a person's beliefs don't match with the truth of the Bible, then that person is following a god of their own imagination. They deny this by siding with the world and claiming Scripture isn't trustworthy or is simply allegorical storytelling, like little kids' fairy tales. This kind of person will say, "I don't believe a loving God would . . . ," and their answer isn't based on Scripture. They say they don't believe a loving God would do certain things, and the world, with its flawed logic, backs this up without understanding the whole of God's Word. The truth is God's Word. God's Word is truth. Anything else is just making stuff up about God and religion. In fact, it's making up a god as they would like God to be, not trusting God as he is.

There are people who call themselves Christian but just make stuff up. I wouldn't choose that person as one to help me carry my burden (Galatians 6:2). For myself, I'd be looking for a true Christian soldier (Ephesians 6:10-20). If I'm involved in a spiritual battle, I want help from someone armed with truth, not just stuff they made up. It would be like going to war and making a daisy chain on the battlefield. Not me, and I wouldn't recommend it for you either.

There may be parts of the Bible that you don't understand. There are parts of the Bible that I don't understand. That doesn't mean the Bible isn't true or trustworthy. It means there are things I don't understand.

Different church denominations have different practices. It doesn't mean there's one church that's one hundred percent correct, and everyone else is wrong. It means that as sinners putting the words of God in place to the best of our ability, we'll have some difficulties. The only way to tell the difference between difficulty and sin, bad theology, or outright anti-Biblical doctrine is to read the Bible yourself in prayer for understanding. If you still have concerns, Proverbs 27:17 says that *iron sharpens iron*, meaning that discussing concerns with someone of greater faith is a way to sharpen the knowledge and love of God in both of you.

As for secular counseling practice, after years of techniques ranging from the stereotypical Freudian analysis (where someone reclines on a couch) to "empty chair" to "primal scream therapy" (Hahaha! Don't. Venting anger only makes you better at venting anger), we've learned one thing. The primary ingredient to successful therapy is a trusting relationship between the therapist and the client. You have to feel it's safe to share your story with the person in front of you. The Holy Spirit will lead you to that person if you need them in your recovery or if you have no access to a Christian counselor.

If you've experienced trauma, you may find a Christian trained in EMDR – Eye Movement Desensitization and

Reprocessing. This treatment option disrupts neural networks related to trauma.

How's that work?

If you've experienced trauma, EMDR interrupts the parts of your brain that hang on to and re-live it. Trauma doesn't have to be something as dramatic as witnessing a murder. Trauma is relative to age, experience, circumstances, etc. If you've experienced trauma, you may have memories that arise when you don't want them to. You may have leftover emotions that overwhelm you when you're in a similar situation. For example, if you got lost in a department store as a child, you may later find yourself in a similar section of a department store with similar sounds and smells and feel intense grief or panic. If that were an isolated incident, you might simply say, "I'm never shopping there again." But sometimes trauma plays into so many situations and circumstances that it makes it very hard to live in the present.

Victims are very often ashamed of having been a victim.

I've been blessed to watch a few EMDR therapy sessions. In one, a guest of the conference volunteered a work situation that could be addressed with EMDR to demonstrate to the rest of us. Her situation was that she had been moved to a new office, and her new co-workers weren't welcoming.

If you've ever been on the receiving end of rejection, you know this is painful. You know that it takes a great measure of strength and courage to stay positive and work well in an unwelcoming environment. Chances are you know that even if God sees your efforts, the situation itself is miserable. Did this work situation count as trauma? Well, for the woman who volunteered, it did. She felt rejected. She also felt ashamed.

The shame is hard to get at. Victims are very often ashamed of having been a victim. We think we should have known better, or we shouldn't have gotten into a certain situation to start with. In the workplace or in a family relationship where there is abuse or rejection, shame is compounded because it can feel as if things will never change because the situation has gone on for so long and "they" – the others – will never change.

Too true. Others may never change willingly. But if you change, others will be forced to change in response to you. If you feel ashamed for being in a situation where you've allowed someone to treat you poorly, you lose your self-respect. The shame and loss of self-respect combine to form a kind of paralysis, because change is hard. It requires you to be brave. People feeling shame struggle to find the courage to work on a bad situation.

I watched this woman shed tears of shame for going into a situation day after day, feeling rejected and disrespected and doing nothing about it. She was moved to tears of joy, though, as she realized her co-workers' behavior said nothing about her. Their response to her was not truth about who she was or how well she did her work.

She was able to picture herself making reasonable requests despite her co-workers' attitudes. She could see herself reasonably expecting good, work-related results in a timely manner. When the session was over, she stood a little taller and smiled a little more brightly. When it was over, she looked forward to going in to work for the first time in more than a year.

The most exciting thing about EMDR is that the changes are long lasting. It disrupts your ability to access the bad memories and feelings and continually replay them. Remember we talked about not hanging on to bad stuff as though you need to keep your guard up forever? Remember how we discussed how the Holy Spirit will guide you? EMDR limits your ability to hang on to bad stuff like the details of traumatic events. It also limits your ability to cast yourself in an unreasonably negative role in any given situation.

The reason it's important to know for sure whether the therapist believes in the authority of the Word of God is that you both have to agree on what to work on letting go of. There are things God may want you to remember. There are things we need to not forget because we have a tendency to repeat them.

Unfortunately, when it comes to EMDR, too few therapists, let alone genuine believers, are trained in it. If you can't find a true Christian therapist trained in EMDR, I would pray that God would lead you to the right person and in turn lead that person in ways most helpful to you.

If not counseling, you may believe the best place to begin formal treatment is with a psychiatrist or physician who can address health issues. A psychiatrist or physician may want to prescribe medication, and there are indeed medications that can be helpful in the early stages of recovery. If you've never taken prescribed drugs for depression **Anti-depressants are not happy pills.** or anxiety or other disorders, however, you should know that some of the medications take weeks to become effective while the side effects can be almost immediate. Some people respond very well to medication while others don't. Some medications have more serious side effects than others.

The most important thing is to be able to discuss your concerns with your psychiatrist or physician and to have realistic expectations. Anti-depressants are not happy pills. Anti-anxiety meds can leave you feeling numb. There are drugs for opiate and narcotic addictions that help curb the cravings enough, so you can focus on recovery. There are medications that help with obsessive thoughts and compulsive behaviors. Some medications cost hundreds of dollars a month while others that have been around for a while are available for much less.

If you're given a prescription, ask questions. Graciously and kindly ask what you can expect, what the dangers are, what happens if you stop taking the drug, and why the prescriber believes this is the best drug for you. Most importantly, before the doctor gets too invested in writing the prescription, you must bravely ask if there are lifestyle changes you could make instead of taking a pill.

I'm not a fan of starting out with the assumption of being on medication forever. I'm not a fan of staying on medication any longer than necessary. I'm also not a fan of avoiding appropriate medications that have tremendous potential to help.

Treatment in general is both art and science. Even strictly biblical counselors follow a studied program of counseling, which is science – that is, an organized body of knowledge. The art is reflected in the grace and timing and understanding of the therapist who could be a counselor, social worker, marriage and family therapist, or pastor. Sometimes clients are desperate to know the *why* of their situation. Why did something happen? Why did I become addicted to this when others don't? Why am I having trouble letting this go? The answer is that everyone has a free will and our world is broken by wrong choices (sin). This isn't a very satisfying answer, but why something happened isn't nearly as important as what you plan to do about it. Letting go of a need to know can be healing.

The medical model of addiction is to say that it's a disease. Some people think calling it a disease means the addict takes no responsibility. To them, the idea is the addicted person can say, "Hey, not my fault, I have a disease!" Realistically, though, calling it a disease means recognizing something must be done. If you're diabetic and do nothing, eventually you'll start decaying and losing limbs. If you have an addiction and do nothing, eventually you'll lose all relationships worth having, your job, or your life. Calling addiction a disease in this age means government and insurance money is set aside to provide help (treatment) for people with this problem to learn the skills to live differently.

No one sets out to develop an addiction. I never met a person who developed an addiction during a time when they were surrounded by loving friends and family, enjoyed their job, were happy with their status in life, and regularly attended church as a welcome and valued member, leaving all stress at the foot of the cross.

When people love the life they're living, addiction only takes away from it.

Whether you call your addiction a disease, a habit, an obsession, or another sin, if your life isn't filled with love and joy and peace and purpose, then you're missing out. You're still trying to find the good life outside of the Good Lord's design for your life. He who created us knows what's best for us.

Chapter 16

A Final Word

I believe people can change. No one has to hit rock bottom, whatever that means, before they can receive help. God has created us in his image with a design for joyful, intentional living, and that can start now. Today. This minute.

As you grow in faith and obedience to God, the Holy Spirit will lead you on a path that uses the gifts Christ Jesus gave you to bless others. The Holy Spirit will lead you to serve others. You'll become more like Jesus, who said, *For even the Son of Man came not to be served but to serve, and to give his life as a ransom for many* (Mark 10:45). As you serve others, you'll find joy and peace and a sense of purpose and fulfillment.

The Holy Spirit won't lead you to seek your own happiness. *But seek first the kingdom of God and his righteousness, and all these things will be added to you* (Matthew 6:33). What things? Things your heavenly Father knows you need as well as things he wants to bless you with, so you can enjoy them and use them to bless others. Like what? Well, that's the exciting part. You have to wait like a little kid to find out what your heavenly Father has in store for you!

Just as we're both saints and sinners when we've confessed Jesus as Lord, persons with addictions can be both extremely selfish and horrifically self-destructive. These are two sides of the coin that make recovery challenging, each in its own way. The selfish part of us never wants to endure the discomfort of too much change. Issues of pride also get in the way of changing selfish behavior to humble and loving behavior. The self-destructive part makes it tempting to give up on the work of recovery, thinking "I'm too damaged" or "I've caused too much damage." The addicted brain will go with either view, since both of them quickly lead to using again.

> God created you with a purpose beyond being an example of what not to do.

The Enemy will use your guilt and shame to urge you towards self-destruction. The Enemy will also use your pride to urge you towards selfish refusal to do the work of recovery. The Enemy will tell you your loved ones aren't worth the effort, and your selfish nature will agree. The Enemy will tell you your life is so worthless recovery doesn't matter, and the urge towards self-destruction will accept this as an excuse to keep using.

There are support groups that can freely and frequently help you resist the lures of the Father of Lies. God created you with a purpose beyond being an example of what not to do. He created you for loving relationships, first with Himself and then with countless others. Support groups include traditional, anonymous groups, and there are newer, faith-based groups rooted in God's Word.

If you find a support group, know this does not replace regular church attendance. The Holy Spirit will nudge you to join a church if you don't attend already. Support groups are where you meet new people in recovery. Church is where you grow in faith and fellowship and increase your understanding of the Word of God. Pray for the Holy Spirit to lead you to the right church for you. Pray to be loving and tender-hearted towards those you encounter.

We're nearing the end of our talk together here. If you're not willing to make the kinds of changes in your life that are required to go forward in recovery, then please consider the extent to which you are holding your loved ones emotionally hostage. If you're not willing to do whatever it takes to recover, then it seems your pride is more important to you than your spouse or your children or your parents. If your sense of dignity means you're going to do the barest minimum to be able to say you're "working on it" so you still receive benefit from your family – don't. Don't give recovery a half-hearted effort.

Love is love's reward. Love is all it's cracked up to be. If you let him, God will make you a tender-hearted fool who cries over commercials for greeting cards and hugs every relative twice. And you'll love him all the more for it. What's more, you'll love your friends and family with such a deep love that you can only be swamped with grateful joy when you hear of their eternal salvation. God will use your transformed life for his glory and testimony if you let him. Put the things in place to allow it to happen. Read your Bible daily. Be honest and brave. *The Lord is not slow to fulfill his promise as some count slowness, but is patient toward you, not wishing that any should perish, but that all should reach repentance* (2 Peter 3:9).

Meet the Author

Elizabeth A. Shartle, Esq., PCC-S, is a licensed attorney building a law practice in Ohio, where thousands of families have been devastated by the opiate epidemic. She is also a licensed professional clinical counselor with a master's degree from Liberty University. Prior to law school, she spent years counseling clients who struggled with substance abuse, addiction, and other mental health disorders. She now provides legal counsel in areas where addiction, mental health, and the law intersect.

Connect with Elizabeth: www.elizabethsoffice.com

Similar Titles

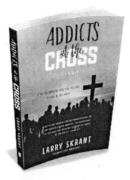

Addicts at the Cross, by Larry Skrant

Addicts at the Cross takes a bold, unabashed stance in stating that the Bible is true: *If the Son therefore shall make you free, ye shall be free indeed* (John 8:36). The 9 steps will walk students to the cross where Christ sets the captives free. These steps aren't magic, but a willing and determined pursuit of freedom through them will guide the student to a place where overcoming addiction is possible.

Society tells us poverty, lack of education, and unemployment are the underlying causes of addiction. Though strong families and education are vital supports for a stable society as they help a person discover how to act and what to do, the roots of addiction develop and grow from "who" the person is. This 9 step study is designed to dredge up the soil of the addict's heart and uproot the underlying causes of addiction, thereby genuinely setting the addict free.

Available where books are sold.

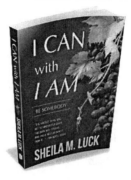

I Can With I AM, by Sheila M. Luck

"Somebody should do something about that!" We hear it and say it frequently. Maybe we have felt that the "somebody" needed to be somebody else because we were not capable, we didn't have the financial or influential means, or that we just didn't have the time; but maybe God wanted us to be that "somebody." Maybe He wants you to be "somebody" today. With God, we can be "somebody." When we work with Him according to His plan, He will provide the abilities and the means. Discover the possibilities. Be somebody! I will do what I can, where I am, with "I AM."

Available where books are sold.

The Overcoming Life, by Dwight L. Moody

Are you an overcomer? Or, are you plagued by little sins that easily beset you? Even worse, are you failing in your Christian walk, but refuse to admit and address it? No Christian can afford to dismiss the call to be an overcomer. The earthly cost is minor; the eternal reward is beyond measure.

Dwight L. Moody is a master at unearthing what ails us. He uses stories and humor to bring to light the essential principles of successful Christian living. Each aspect of overcoming is looked at from a practical and understandable angle. The solution Moody presents for our problems is not religion, rules, or other outward corrections. Instead, he takes us to the heart of the matter and prescribes biblical, God-given remedies for every Christian's life. Get ready to embrace genuine victory for today, and joy for eternity.

Available where books are sold.

CPSIA information can be obtained
at www.ICGtesting.com
Printed in the USA
FFOW02n0518190218
45125494-45582FF